OLD TIME TALLAHASSEE
FROM A TO Z

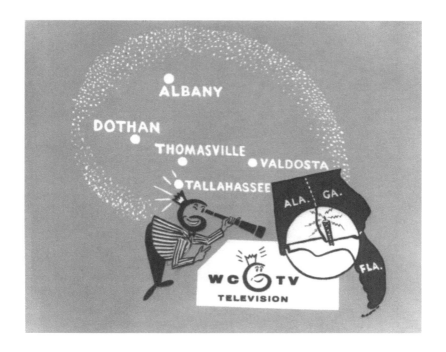

J. Kent Thompson

Mural on the back of the Leon County Courthouse

FROM THE AUTHOR

This book is by no means all inclusive. It is based on my memories and experiences living in, and loving Tallahassee. I hope as you walk down memory lane with me it will bring back a time that was a lot simpler than today. The photographs used in this book are from my personal collection and the State Archives of Florida, Florida Memory Project. Years ago, there was a sign painted on the side of Quailty Dry Cleaners located at West College Avenue and Duval Street that read *"Isn't it great to live in Tallahassee."* I whole-heartedly believe it is. If you would like to share some places you remember that could be included in later updates, I would love to hear from you. I can be contacted at jkt416@gmail.com.

Dedicated to my mother:

Bettye
who loved Tallahassee and its history,
1922-2005

TABLE OF CONTENTS

A

Acme Dairies was a group of local dairies that joined together to sell their products. It consisted of the Hartsfield, Leon and Sellers dairies.

Alford Brothers Men's Wear was located at 212 South Monroe. It was a popular place to buy the white long sleeve shirts that businessmen wore until the mid- sixties when colored shirts came into vogue.

Alford Chevrolet was a car dealership located at 327 North Adams and later 2323 N. Monroe.

Alumni Village off Lake Bradford Road was a residence facility for married college students with children, that attended Florida State University.

AM Radio Stations before the advent of FM radio, all we had were AM stations. Tallahassee's first was WTAL which was initially broadcast from a house on the corner of Betton and Thomasville Road, then from the Cherokee Hotel, then from 533 East Tennessee, and 2343 Phillips Road. Tallahassee's second radio station WTNT 1450 broadcast from the Floridan Hotel in the early 1950's, then later the Duval Hotel. Other stations were WMEN broadcasting out of the Floridan Hotel and WRFB broadcasting from Lakeshore Drive.

Angelo's Restaurant was located at 129 North Monroe and was a popular lunch spot for downtown office workers.

1

Annette's Woman's Apparel at 113 East College served the fairer sex for years with the latest fashions.

A&P Grocery had two locations in town, one originally at 328 North Adams (on NE corner of Adams and College) that moved to 1015 North Monroe, and another at 1105 East Lafayette (where The Moon is today.)

Apalachee Parkway is the name of the highway leading from the Capital. It was completed in 1957 and became a part of U.S. 27.

Apalachee Parkway Shoppes opened in 1950. It was the beginning of change for Tallahassee from downtown shopping to shopping in a mall. Although the stores were spread out in the shopping center, buyers could find all their needs met at one stop.

Apex Linen Service at 606 West 4th Avenue supplied clean linen service to Tallahassee hotels and motels as well as steady employment to many.

Area codes were a numbering code developed by AT&T in 1947 to determine geographic zones for phone numbers. Originally all of Florida was 305. Due to growth, the area north of Tampa and Orlando, including Tallahassee, was split off and given the 904 area code in 1966. In 1998 the panhandle area west of Jacksonville was changed to 850.

Arnold's Boy's Wear was the "in" place to shop for children's clothes. It was located at 104 South Monroe.

Arthur Murray Dance Studio at 109 ½ East College was where residents went to learn all the new dances of the sixties such as the Hully Gully, Bird, Limbo, the Locomotion, and ballroom dancing.

Ashmore's Drug Store *"We Are Small But We Have it All"* at 509 West Brevard Street was an institution in Tallahassee. Owned by Robert Ashmore, all of the hopeful candidates for Governor would stop by for good luck. He bought pecans from the residents of Frenchtown and was a friend to all. It closed in 2007.

B

Bagel Peddler was the first bagel shop in Tallahassee. Originally located at 1885-1 North Boulevard across from the Northwood Mall, they introduced Tallahassee to bagels. Before it went out of business it moved to a few other locations around town.

Bakers Pharmacy served the south side of town and was located at 1815 South Adams across from Florida A&M University.

Banjo's Smokehouse was a place to get good barbeque in Tallahassee. Located at 2325 Apalachee Parkway it was run by "Red." It closed in 2008 and reopened as the Silver Bullet Diner. Today it is the location of **Jason's Deli**.

The Bargain Box was located at 123 North Monroe Street. It sat next to the library when it was located in the old Elks Club building.

Barnaby's is a still popular pizza restaurant in Tallahassee. They once had two locations, one in front of the Northwood Mall on North Monroe and the current store on the Apalachee Parkway. Friends still gather there to eat good pizza and drink a pitcher of beer or soda.

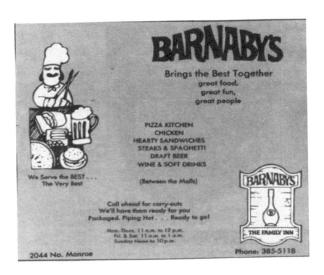

Barnacle Bills' was a local seafood restaurant and oyster bar located on North Monroe Street. Famous for steamed seafood and oysters on the half shell, their catchy phrase *"You know where — Barnacle Bill's on North Monroe"* has a way of sticking in your head and making you want to return again and again. It closed after a catastrophic fire in 2016.

Barnacle Bill's
RESTAURANT & LOUNGE
Florida Seafood

Bay Gas Station was located near the Perry Drive-In on the parkway. I remember as a kid watching the sign slowly flash each letter B-A-Y then remain lighted showing the word BAY for a few seconds before starting over again.

Belk Shoes was located on Monroe Street next to J.C. Penny's in the 1950's.

Beer Growing up in Tallahassee you quickly learned where teens could buy beer. Places like Smitty's, Big Oaks, and Gardner's Grocery were but a few.

Bellflower Marine used to be located at 2010 South Monroe before it moved out to Highway 20.

Bennett's Drug Store opened in 1937. Located at 200 South Monroe on the southwest corner of College and Monroe, they filled prescriptions and sold sundry items. Their lunch counter and booths were always crowded with college students and locals for lunch or just to meet and have a cherry vanilla coke and French fries. You could select songs to play on the jukebox from a box on your table. It closed in 1976.

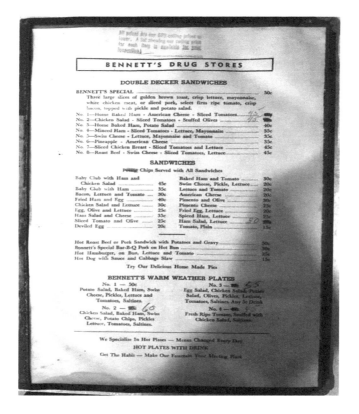

Benson's Jewelers was located at 214 South Monroe.

Bertha Cooke's a woman's dress shop was located at 206 West College and later at 304 South Monroe St.

Bevis Funeral Home is a local funeral home founded in 1964 by Russell Bevis and now run by his son Rocky. Longtime residents remember when the business was located on the southeast corner of Thomasville Road and Sixth Avenue. Later the Chez Pierre Restaurant, Front Porch, and now Table 23 is located there.

Biff Burgers was a hamburger business located at 1020 West Pensacola Street. They offered hamburgers that were *"Roto Broiled."*

Bill's Bookstore located at 107 South Copeland has been an institution in Tallahassee for years. They specialize in selling text books and memorabilia to Florida State University students.

Bird Cage Tea Room was located in the Northwood Mall.

Black Cat News Exchange was located at 115 N. Monroe on the east side of Monroe between Park & College. It was a popular news-stand and book store for years.

Black's Pony Rides were operated by the Black family. Many a Tallahassee child's birthday party was made special by the arrival of the trailer bearing his ponies. Children would ride the ponies around the yard or house led by Mr. Black and his family.

Blalock's Jewelers was located at 113 West College Avenue.

Blount's Plumbing was owned by Walter Blount. His store was located in an old filling station near the intersection of Monroe and Thomasville Roads. He installed a drinking fountain outside the door and a placed sign over the fountain that advertised *"Free Ice Cold Water."*

Blue Sink was a popular swimming hole located off the Crawfordville Highway. It was also a favorite spot to go parking with your date. In the 60s it was the scene of a horrific double murder of two teenage girls. It is now closed to the public.

Body Electric was a 1984 fitness and aerobics program on PBS hosted by Margaret Richards. From its start on Tallahassee's WFSU TV it became a national sensation. Its opening song was "I Sing the Body Electric" based on an 1855 poem from *Leaves of Grass*. Local women and students were featured exercising and following Richards instruction.

Borden's Dairy was located at 1945 North Monroe. Prior to Borden's the site was home to Bassett's Dairy. In the late 50's and 60's drivers would load their trucks in the morning with milk products packed in ice chips to deliver to the front door of homes throughout Tallahassee. I had a friend who stayed out too late one night and was able to catch a ride home with the "Milkman" as he made his rounds the next morning.

Bottling Companies:
Dr. Pepper Bottling Company was at 306 North Copeland,
Double Cola at 694 ½ Industrial Drive,
Pepsi & 7 Up was at 311 E. Jennings,
Royal Crown Cola was at 210 E. Oakland.
Coca Cola was in the Mayco Building at 1320 South Monroe. It used to have a bush shaped like a coke bottle out front.

Bowman's Auto Court was called Clarks Deluxe Auto Courts before the 1950's. It was located at 1925 North Monroe Street. They offered 50 cottages and advertised themselves as *"A home away from home."* Bowman's also had a liquor store, a lounge called the *Tally-Ho*, and a restaurant. They were famous for their homemade biscuits and orange marmalade jelly. A Skaggs - Albertson's store was later built on the property. Today it houses a fitness club.

Bradley's Country Store Bradley's on Centerville Road in the Felkel community has been selling sausage since 1910. The store building was built in 1927. Selling smoked sausage and milled grits the store has become a local legend. People ship Bradley's sausages all over the world to share their delicious treat with friends. You can stop by and get a soft drink and a 12" sausage dog, a porkchop sandwich, or a bacon, lettuce, and tomato sandwich, then sit in the rocking chairs out front and enjoy.

Brothers Three Big Daddy's Lounge was a popular night scene for students. Friends would meet there to drink, dance and be seen. It was located off the parkway in the shopping center near present day Blair Stone Road.

Brown Derby was a popular steak restaurant and bar in the early 70's. Designed to look like an English pub it was located behind the Tallahassee Mall near John Knox Road.

Brown's Men's Wear was located at 100 South Monroe. They specialized in suits, shirts and fashionable ties. The Florida Association of Counties is now located there.

Brown's Pharmacy was located at 441 North Monroe. In the fifties they would deliver your prescription to your home. A black gentleman named Johnny would deliver them on his three-wheeled Cushman motorcycle. Behind the seat sat a large metal box that held his deliveries. Sometimes if he was not too rushed to make deliverie's he would ride the neighborhood kids around the block on his motorcycle. They opened a second store in the Northwood Mall.

Buddy's Hardware and Sporting Goods at 203 South Monroe Street was where teams went to get their uniform shirts printed as well as sports equipment.

Bullwinkle's Saloon a popular bar and night spot for college students, has been open since 1979. Located at 620 West Tennessee Street near the campus it is part of the famed "*Tennessee Waltz*" that students, when turning the legal drinking age, make celebrating their newfound independence and first legal drink. Rated as one of the top 100 college bars, it is usually packed with FSU students.

Burdines Drug Store had two locations in Tallahassee, one at 206 South Adams Street and the other at 1567 Thomasville Road. The Thomasville Road store later moved to 1815-2 in the Miracle Plaza.

Burger Chef was located on the Apalachee Parkway and touted their own special sauce.

Bus Stations Two locations served bus customers in the early days of Tallahassee. The Trailway's Bus Station at 318 North Monroe and the Greyhound Stations at 113 South Adams and Tennessee Street. It opened in 1943. Later the two were combined into the station at Adams and Tennessee.

Busy Bee Café was located at 106 South Monroe Street and was a popular hangout in the 1940's.

Butler's Shoes located at 224 South Monroe was where most women shopped for shoes in downtown Tallahassee.

B&W Fruit Market was a popular produce stand located at 1208 South Monroe just past the railroad underpass. I remember going there when I was a kid to buy fruit to make hand churned ice-cream and bushel hampers of green peanuts to boil and sell at the local swimming pools.

Through the years the B&W Fruit Market located on S. Monroe, suffered through a devastating fire and occasional local flooding.

Byrd's Grocery also called T.B. Byrd and Son, was located first on Monroe Street, then at 211 East Tennessee Street and later moved to 1101 Thomasville Road. Advertised as *"Tallahassee Oldest Grocery,"* it started business in the early 1800's. They offered a unique blend of roasted coffee that was prized by locals and had their own coffee grinder. The store also had peanut butter and mayonnaise making machines. The store was the first in Tallahassee to have a telephone and its phone number was #1. The store closed in 1965.

C

Camellia Bakery was located at 617 North Monroe Street. We used to go there to get fresh doughnuts, cream horns, and radio rings. They advertised themselves as *"Tallahassee's Finest"* and for years they were.

Canopy Roads are located throughout Tallahassee. Oaks line the roads offering respite from the heat and a chance to forget where you are for just a moment. There are five designated canopy roads in Tallahassee:

- <u>Miccosukee Road</u> from Capital Circle Northeast to Moccasin Gap.
- <u>Centerville Road</u> from Seventh Avenue, merges with Moccasin Gap road to County Road 59.
- <u>Meridian Road</u> Seventh Avenue to Georgia state line.
- <u>Old Bainbridge Road</u> from Raa Avenue to Capital Circle northwest.
- <u>Old St. Augustine Road</u> south of Governor's Square to W.W. Kelly Road.

Capitol Building Tallahassee was named Florida's capital in 1824. The first capitol building was a log cabin. It was replaced in 1826 but torn down in 1839. The third capitol, built in 1845, was improved with a dome and two wings in 1902. Other improvements occurred in 1923, 36, and 47. The new 22 story capitol opened in 1977. The old capitol reopened in April of 1986 and now serves as a museum.

Capital City First National Bank at 217 North Monroe was on the southeast corner of Monroe and Tennessee Streets and could be identified by its large time and temperature sign. Besides going inside to bank you could go around the back to the walk-up teller booth. Later they built drive-up teller booths across the street. Mert Ashcroft ran day to day operations for Mr. Godfrey Smith. Ann Monk was the Head Teller.

Capital Circle called the *"truck route"* by the locals; it originally was designed to serve as a by-pass for trucks going through Tallahassee. It was completed December 11, 1963. With the growth of Tallahassee, it has now become a major traffic artery for people traveling around Tallahassee.

Capital City Lumber used to be located at 604 West Gaines Street. They have been providing hardware and lumber to Tallahassee for many years. They later moved to 2501 Lonnbaldh Road.

Capital Drive-In Theater opened in the 1950's and was located at Four Points on Woodville Highway across from Tuckers Drive-In. It had one screen and the lot held 300 cars. We would go there to watch B movies like "The Attack of the 50 Foot Women," "The Blob," Audie Murphy war movies, and westerns. Popcorn, drinks and snacks were available at the concession stand located towards the back of the parking lot. You would drive up to the speakers and place one on your rolled down window to listen to the sound of the movie. Many a time you drove off with a speaker, forgetting it was there (or on purpose.) Those who came to the movie with things other than a movie on their mind would park in the back rows and it would not be too long before the windows steamed up! The theater was closed in the 1970's and in the 80's the screen burned down. The land was later cleared and today it serves as a holding pond.

Capital Field was the name given to the football field built behind the fairgrounds off of South Monroe Street. Before high schools built stadiums on their property, all of their football games were played there.

Capital Plaza was the group of stores at 1838 Thomasville Road. It was once called Setzer's Plaza after the grocery there.

Capital Shoe Fixery at 118 East Jefferson always smelled of shoe polish. You would drop off your shoes to be re-soled. They always came back shined and looking like new. It is now located on S. Magnolia.

Captain Louie's Galley was also known as Louis Seafare. Selling seafood boxes to go, their advertisements promised *"A Banquet in a Box."* They were located at 620 West Tennessee Street.

Cardboard Boxes were all a kid needed to have a good time when you lived near Leon and Cobb Schools. The hills in front of Leon and around the Cobb bowl provided all you needed for a fun ride. Big refrigerator boxes were good, but even a small piece of cardboard would do.

Carriage Shop at 931 North Monroe sold the latest in women's fashion.

Caroline Brevard Elementary School was built in 1924 and was originally located downtown at 727 South Calhoun Street. Named after a local teacher, the original art deco building is also known as the Bloxham Building. It was recently refurbished. The school moved to 2006 Jackson Bluff Road in 1959 and is no longer used as an elementary school but instead houses the S.A.I.L. program.

Carousel Restaurant at 318 North Monroe was a longtime favorite where people went to eat in town.

Carters Sporting Goods was located at 119 South Adams and supplied baseball gloves to many a growing kid in Tallahassee.

Cemeteries Tallahassee has 89; the Old City Cemetery holds Tallahassee pioneers and governors including Prince and Princess Murat, Greenwood- Willie Galimore, Culley's Meadow Wood- Dean Chenoweth, Michael J. Shaara, Oakland- Claude Pepper, Roselawn Paul Dirac, Southside- Cannonball Adderley, Memory Gardens- Dick Howser.

Centennial Field was built in 1924 to celebrate Tallahassee's first 100 years (Centennial.) The perimeter of the field was lined with limestone walls. It has been home to Leon High Football games, and a semi-pro baseball team. From 1947-50 the FSU Seminole's played their football games there (they lost the first one to Stetson). Babe Ruth Baseball games, inter-city flag football, and school intramural games were also played there. It also served as a venue for wrestling matches. I remember going to see "*The American Dream*" Dusty Rhodes there.

From the early 1900 to the 1950's a City Gas Manufacturing plant was located on the southern corner of the property. Waste from the gas making process deposited into the ground contaminated it. The site was closed in 1974 and the waste later removed. The land sat vacant for many years. With funding from a penny sales tax increase the City of Tallahassee revitalized the area.

They built a park and greenway for the citizens called **Cascade's Park** which opened in 2014. A walking trail and amphitheater are located there as well as a pictorial remembrance to the old Smokey Hollow community that used to be located there. The park also is the location of Florida's **Prime Meridian** marker, the foundation point for all land mapping. The gas plant building was restored and now serves as the **Edison** restaurant. The park was named after the old cascades falls that were there when the city was chosen to be the Capitol city in 1824.

Chanelo's Pizza House was a pizza parlor located at 618 West Tennessee Street. They advertised "*pies made to order*." Chanelo's and Tony's were the first take-out pizza places in town.

Chandlers Hamburgers was an answer to McDonalds. Hamburgers were advertised as being "*Served Quick as a Wink*." Two franchises were located in town. One was at 628 North Monroe (now a Budget Rental Center) and the other at 1825 South Adams.

Charley Mac's was located off I-10 and Thomasville road. They served bread sticks and a Sunday brunch featuring omelets to order and Belgian waffles.

Charles Chips had *"more real potato taste,"* and were sold door to door in their distinctive yellow and brown cans in the early 1970's. The tasty chips with their regular, barbeque, and jalapeno flavors were a welcome treat for buyers used to buying their chips in bags that had a little charcoal filter bag enclosed to keep them fresh. The Charles Chip man would come every week to sell you a refill can. They also sold cookies and pretzels. You can still buy them at Cracker Barrel stores.

Cherokee Hotel was built in the mid 1920s on the southwest corner of Calhoun Street and Park Avenue next to the Walker Library. It was managed by J.A. Stiles. The Montgomery Ward and Co. store used to operate out of the hotel at one time. Years after the hotel was closed, we used to climb the fire escapes on a dare. It was torn down in 1964.

Chevet's Photo Supply at 200 South Adams was the place to go to get your pictures developed in town.

Chick "n" Treat was a popular place to get fried chicken sandwiches. It was located at 1215 Apalachee Parkway.

Chi Omega is an FSU sorority house on Park Avenue. It was the scene of a grisly double murder by serial killer Ted Bundy on Jan 15, 1978. He also severely beat two other coeds and another woman a few blocks away that same night. He was captured in Pensacola, Florida in February of 1978. He was tried and convicted and sentenced to die in Florida's electric chair. His execution was January 24, 1989.

Christmas lights used to be strung across Monroe Street. In a scene reminiscent of *The Christmas Story*, they were red, green, blue, and orange bulbs on wires. When the Mormon Church on Stadium Drive was constructed it became one of the must-see places to view Christmas lights. The buildings and trees would be decorated in thousands of lights and cars would drive through their parking lot gawking at their beauty.

Christos was a department store located at 208 South Monroe.

Chuck E. Cheese was located in the Sugar Mill Plaza. It opened in the 1980's and offered two levels with video games, a pizza parlor, and climbing equipment, nets, tubes and slides as well as a pit filled with multi-colored balls to swim and play in. Kids would have their birthday parties there and be visited by a person dressed in a big Chuck E. Cheese costume. There is still one in Tallahassee today on Sharer Road.

Circle K stores are some of the latest in a long line of convenience stores in Tallahassee.

Churches Tallahassee has many old churches. Trinity United Methodist is the oldest, started in 1824. The oldest building still standing is the First Presbyterian Church built 1835-38. Saint John's Episcopal original building was built in 1829 but burned down and was replaced in the late 1800s. Pisgah United Methodist was started in 1830 and its current structure built in 1858. First Baptist was organized in 1849. Though the Catholic Church has been represented in the Tallahassee area since the 1500s, the first Catholic Church was built in 1845 on the northeast corner of Park and Gadsden Streets.

City Hall built in 1892, was originally at corner of Adams Street and Park Avenue. The city fire station was located under the building on the road. It was demolished in 1963 and the seat of city government was moved to the Martin Building on Adams. In 1981 the Martin Building was torn down and a new (current) city hall was built on the property.

City Jail was on Gaines Street. Later called the George Firestone Building, it was torn down in 2018 to make way for new development. A large oak tree still stands beside the road and is known as the *"Hanging Tree."* In 1909 Mick Morris, a black man who had shot and killed Leon County Sheriff Morris Langston, was hung there by a mob.

Old City Jail

City Limit markers used to be on Fourth Avenue near Oakland cemetery and on Meridian north of John Knox Road.

City of Tallahassee supply barn was located off of Gaines and Meridian. The warehouse was used to store all the supply needs of the city workers. Crews would meet up there in the morning to load their trucks and go out on the job.

Civic Center the *"Donald L. Tucker Leon County Civic Center,"* is simply called the Civic Center by most. Few even remember that Tucker was a former area legislator and Speaker of the House of Representatives. It opened on September 14, 1981.

Clock Tower Located at 815 South Macomb Street was built in 1910. It was designed by New York architect Calvin C. Phillips. He had also designed buildings for the 1889 Paris World's Fair. He moved to Tallahassee and lived on St. Michael Street. The clock tower was auctioned off in 1974 by the Heritage Foundation to the Madison Center, an investment firm. It was torn down sometime in the 1980's.

The Coffee Pot was a popular a drive-in located at 1208 North Monroe Street in the 1930's.

Collin's Furniture was located at 105 South Monroe and later moved to 1117 Thomasville Road.

Confederate Inn was a supper club located at the Ochlocknee River on the "new" Quincy Highway. The big dance floor was a popular spot to hold parties.

Columns also known as the William *"Money"* Williams mansion was built in 1830. Williams was a banker who established the Union Bank and legend has it that a nickel was placed in each brick used to build the house. The old Tallahassee Antebellum house originally sat on the corner of Adams Street and Park Avenue. It served as the home to the Dutch Kitchen Restaurant before being used as the first home to the Leon County Public Library in 1956. A basement was used for the children's section. When the library moved to the old Elks Club building on Monroe Street it became a coffee shop. The building was moved in 1971 to its present site at 100 North Duval Street on the old Leon High School property next to the LeRoy Collins library. It was once home to the Chamber of Commerce but now is owned by the James Madison Institute. Legend has it that the building is haunted by the ghost of Rebecca Bailey who once lived there. She has been seen searching the building for her husband who did not return from the Civil War.

The Columns

Core's Grocery was located at 620 West Ninth Avenue but later moved to 1627 North Boulevard across from Augusta Raa Junior High. Kids would come into the small store to spend their lunch money on candy before school. Special treats were the Woo-Wee wax whistles and wax lips as well as Flavor Aid in a straw.

The Corral Drive-In was located at 1621 South Monroe. The female car hops were dressed in tight, revealing outfits that caused all the boys in town to want to come there to eat and girl watch.

Country Club subdivision was Tallahassee's second platted neighborhood, built after Los Robles in 1926. It was once considered the home to Tallahassee's elite before the flight to the suburbs of Killearn. The Capital City Country Club, a golf course and club house is also in the subdivision.

Cox Furniture at 2209 Thomasville Rd sold upscale furniture to residents for years.

Crow's Nest was a popular beer joint where locals liked to meet and play foosball. Located off of Lake Bradford Road, it was firebombed April 4, 1968, the night Martin Luther King Jr. was assassinated. The owner's son, Travis Crow, was still inside and perished.

Culley's J.A. Culley and Son's Undertakers at 210 E. Pensacola provided burial and ambulance services.

Curb Market a place to sell local farm produce, has been located in many places in Tallahassee. In 1827-8 it was located in Wayne Square where the current Tallahassee City Hall is located. Locals called the place Rascal Square after the horse and mule trading that went on there. The city built a market house there for the traders to sell their wares every day from dawn to dark except Sunday. Fire in 1843 and a storm in 1846 destroyed the buildings.

A new building was erected on Park Avenue across from the First Presbyterian Church. In the 1920's the curb market was moved to Fishers Green on South Boulevard Street across from Immanuel Baptist Church. Hours were limited to Wednesdays and Saturday mornings.

In the 1930's before the Martin Building was constructed (where city hall is today) the market was moved to that site on South Adams.

In 1942 the market moved to East Gaines Street next to the city jail. Vendors were housed under a pavilion that had stalls where they could lay out their wares. The stalls cost $3.00 a year for a full stall and 1.50 a year for a half. The market operated here until 1965.

In 1974 a market was opened at Cascade Park at the Fair Grounds.

In 1984 the Farmers Market was opened at Market Square at 1415 Timberlane Road.

For the past few years a market has also operated in the chain of parks across from the Federal courthouse on Park Avenue not far from its 1846 location. New building construction at the Timberlane site will mean the market will have to move to another location soon.

Curb Market off Gaines and Meridian Streets

Cypress Lounge was located in the Floridan Hotel building.

Old Centennial Field before development of Cascades Park

D

Daffin Theater built by Charles E. Daffin was on Clinton Street (later named College Avenue) it was Tallahassee's first theater, opening in 1912. The name was changed to the **State Theater** in 1932. Earlier Tallahassee theaters were the **Capital Theater** circa 1920s, and the **Ritz,** opened in 1930 by E.J. Sparks.

The Daffin Theater on Clinton St.

The State Theater of College Ave.

The Capital Theater on S. Macomb St.

The Ritz Theater at 108 S. Monroe

Dairy Dream was an ice cream store at 1023 North Monroe. They offered sundaes and cones as well as foot-long chili dogs with onions.

Dale Mabry Field opened in 1929 as Tallahassee's first commercial airport. It was named after a local native and World War I aviator who died in a dirigible crash in 1922. At the time, the crash was the greatest disaster in aeronautics, resulting in 34 deaths.

Dalton's Drugs was located at 1311 Miccosukee Road and served Tallahassee families for years.

Danish Bakery was located at 1541 South Monroe.

Danley Furniture was located at 1919 West Tennessee Street near the Varsity Plaza. It was the Ethan Allen dealer in Tallahassee for years.

Day 'n' Night was a sandwich and coffee shop across from Leon High School at 425 East Tennessee Street.

Day "n" Night Diner was located at 1312 West Tennessee Street and was fashioned after the old roadside diners.

Deeb's Hats 222 E. College owned by William Deeb and Annelle Deeb Humphrey's. The original store was called Deeb's Hat Heaven and was opened in 1905 on Jefferson Street by their parents. They moved to their College Avenue location to give way to the construction of the expanded Capitol complex.

Deep Cut is on Magnolia Drive beside the Tallahassee Democrat building. It was made in 1860 to connect the railroad from Lake City to Tallahassee.

Hernando DeSoto celebrated the first Christmas Mass in what would become the United States right here in Tallahassee in 1539. The site is marked on Desoto Park Drive south of East Lafayette St.

Devil's Dip is the name for the dip in road on Magnolia Drive between Miccosukee Road and East Tennessee Street. Before the road was reconfigured to four lanes in 1976 there was a steep incline between the two hills.

Diana Shop at 124 South Monroe was a woman's dress shop.

Dixie Cream Do-Nuts was located at 210 West College, then at 307 South Adams, and later at 1119 Apalachee Parkway. They lured customers to come in *"For that bite between meals."*

Dixieland Drive-In was located at 1804 South Monroe. A radio station used to broadcast from the parking lot and kids would come to be heard on the radio. The night it snowed in Tallahassee in 1958 they held snowman building contest on the hoods of people's cars.

Dobb's House was a family restaurant located at 685 West Tennessee Street.

Dog Et Al has been around for over 35 years. Started by David Taylor, it changed hands to new owners in March of 2019. You can still get great hotdogs and corn dogs there.

Elinor Doyle has been selling flowers in Tallahassee for many years. They were located at 202 South Adams where the Governors Club is today. After losing their lease to the club, they moved up College Avenue between Monroe and Adams.

Drag Strip located on Highway 20 was called the Seminole Raceway or the Tallahassee Speedway. Opening in the 1960's, it was Tallahassee's attempt at a big time drag strip. A 2700-foot-long stretch of pavement was laid out and cars would drag in front of a grandstand for onlookers. It closed in 1982 but there has been talk of reopening it. The strip is still visible through the fences.

Driftwood Motel at 1402 West Tennessee was just behind the Howard Johnson's ice cream store.

The Driftwood Motel on Brevard & Tennessee Streets

Driving around Tallahassee was easy before people started worrying about security. You could drive around the circular driveway at the Governor's mansion and stop at the front door to ask if the Governor was in (a stern State Trooper would always say *"No!"*) or you drive around the Westcott Fountain and pour soap powder in the water. The advent of soap tablets was hailed by many pranksters because you could drive by and throw them in the fountain without stopping. The old capital was another spot you could drive up to and run in to get a soft drink from the blind woman in the basement concession.

Drive-Ins Tallahassee has had many popular drive-ins from Mutt & Jeff's to the Wagon Wheel. All operated about the same. You would drive into the parking lot, then back into a space and flash your lights. The car-hop, usually a pretty young lady, would come out and take your order. When the order was ready, she would bring it out on a metal tray that would be attached to your car door. You would pay her, and she would make change from a roll of bills in her apron or the coin changer hanging on her waist. The driver would then pass out the food to the occupants of the car and you would sit and eat and watch other cars come into the parking lot. Most are gone today though some still imitate the practice as a theme such as **Sonic**.

Dubey's was a popular bookstore and news-stand in Tallahassee. It was located at 319 South Monroe Street.

Dutch Kitchen restaurant was a local favorite in the 1940's and was located at 102 South Adams in the Columns. They also advertised a tea room.

Duval Hotel opened in 1951 and is located at 415 North Monroe Street. It has changed names and hands a couple of times, once serving as an FSU dormitory, but it was always the Duval Hotel to many. Their bar was named Le Roc and was a favorite watering hole to many legislators and locals. Drakes Massage Studio, a place you could exercise, take a steam bath or get a massage was located in the basement. Today it is refurbished and open once again as the Hotel Duval.

Duval Hotel on Monroe St.

E

East Hill Baptist Church on Miccosukee Road was originally located in a home that had been moved from 202 W. College. It later became the chapel and a new church building stands next to it today.

W.T. Edwards TB Hospital at 2323 Phillips Road was built in 1952 and had 400 beds. It was later taken over by the State of Florida and renamed the **Sunland Center** and was used to house mentally and physically handicapped patients. It was closed in 1983 and sat vacant for years, slowly deteriorating. Local lore had it that there were ghosts there and teenagers would dare each other to go in the building. It was torn down in 2007 and an apartment complex, the Victoria Grand was built on the property.

Ed & Bernice's was a fish camp and restaurant off of Highway 20 at the Lake Talquin Dam. Serving up plates of all you can eat fried catfish; their parking lot was always full on the weekends.

Elberta Crate and Box Company Built in 1922, it was named after the Elberta peach. They initially built crates to ship peaches and tomatoes but later expanded paper overlaid veneer from which expendable pallets were made. The mill was located off of Lake Bradford Road and was a major employer in Tallahassee for many years. When the owners decided to consolidate the Tallahassee operations with the Bainbridge, Georgia facility in 1977, it was closed.

El Chico Grill was a popular spot for the college students. It was located at 609 Osceola Drive.

El Dorado Café advertised itself as *"catering to Colored,"* in pre-integration Tallahassee. It was located at 447 West Virginia Street.

Eighty-Four Lumber was only in Tallahassee for a short time. Located between the truck route and Thomasville Road near I-10 they were the first mega hardware-lumber company to come to Tallahassee.

Elks Lodge at 127 North Monroe later became the second home to the Leon County Public Library. The lodge moved to larger quarters on Magnolia Street. The library would later move to the Northwood Mall. The Tennyson, an apartment complex, is located on the old lodge Monroe Street property today.

Eppes-Edenfield Hardware was located at 1334 North Monroe on the southwest corner of Seventh Avenue across from the old armory. Run by *"Tiny"* Eppes you could spend the day looking through their big nail bins. They sold hardware and paint. Today Dura Print is located there.

Esso Gasoline told us in the sixties to "*Put a tiger in your tank,*" and ran an advertising campaign that gave you a tiger tail to hang from your gas cap along with the bumper-sticker proclaiming, *"I've got a tiger in my tank."* Lots of folks around Tallahassee had a tiger tail on their car.

Exchange Bank building is located on the corner of College and Monroe. It was at one time the tallest structure in Tallahassee. Opened March 3, 1928, it had six floors. For years it has been known as the Midyette-Moore Building.

Exchange Bank 1928

F

F & T restaurant at 113 South Monroe was a favorite for breakfast or lunch. They were famous for their all-meat chili.

Fain Drug Store was located at 119 South Monroe and like Bennett's, had a soda fountain inside.

Faivers Drive-In a popular hang-out for high school kids was located across the street from the Corral on South Monroe.

Faivers Restaurant was located 1312 West Tennessee Street and had a place at the bridge in Panacea.

Fair Grounds consist of 140 acres purchased by the City of Tallahassee for $62,500 on July 31, 1949. It is home to the annual North Florida Fair usually held at the end of October thru the first few days of November. Before amusement parks became common it was a big event in Tallahassee when the fair came to town. Schools would be let out at noon and there would be a "*fair parade.*" Kids would get in free that day.

Fairy Tale Shop 118 1/2 South Monroe sold children clothes. It later moved to 1906 Thomasville Road.

Fallen Officers Unfortunately Tallahassee and Leon County have each lost brave soul's serving the community and keeping us safe.

The **Tallahassee Police Department** has lost five officers in the line of duty, they are:

Sgt Warren T. Gay- 6/8/1981 - Motorcycle accident.
Officer Ernest Ponce DeLeon- 7/8/1988 - Gunfire.
Crossing Guard Ruby R. Roudon- 11/2/1990 – Killed by a passing vehicle.
Sgt. Dale Green- 11/13/2002 – Gunfire.
Officer Michael P. Sanders- 12/12//2009 – Killed by a Hit and Run driver.

The **Leon County Sheriff's Office** has lost three Officers and one K-9:

Sheriff Willie M. Langston- 3/1/1909 – Gunfire
Deputy Khomas C. Revels- 9/18/1970 – Gunfire
Deputy Christopher Lynd Smith 11/22/2014 – Gunfire
K9 Koda 1/31/2013 - Gunfire

Fallschase was going to be a huge subdivision located off of Buck Lake Road in the 1980's. I remember they used to have a balloon festival there. The developers ran into problems with the city who did not want to approve the permits due to environmental concerns. The land sat dormant for years while the legal battles raged. A settlement was made in 2007 and the land now houses a Costco, Walmart, and Outdoor Shop.

Federal Bake Shop at 310 South Monroe was in business for many years before closing.

Federal Courthouse and the downtown Post Office opened on East Park Avenue Jan 18, 1937. The post office later moved out. Prior to the courthouse being built, the old **Leon Hotel** stood on the spot. The hotel burned down in 1925.

Fireworks Fourth of July celebrations were held at Lake Ella off of North Monroe Street until the event got too big for the location. They were last held there in July of 1984. The event moved for a year to the parking lot of the Tallahassee Mall, and then Capital Field at the fairgrounds until it found a permanent home at the new Tom Brown Park.

First Baptist Church was built in 1915. Through the years it has expanded to cover the entire block between College and Park Avenue. In doing so it has built where the old Columns and Union Bank stood.

First Presbyterian Church located at 110 North Adams was built in 1838 and is the oldest public building in Tallahassee. It is the last standing church built during Florida's Territorial days.

Five Points are the intersections of Thomasville Road, Meridian Road and Seventh Avenue at the gates of Los Robles. It was called this until the roads were diverted to ease congestion in the area in 2000.

Fleets Department Store was located first at 102 East Jefferson Street, then at 210 South Monroe.

Flemings School of Dance at 117 North Calhoun was operated by Mildred Fleming. She taught many a young girl ballet and other types of dance through the years.

Florida High the FSU experimental school was located on Stadium Drive. Originally it was called the *"Demonstration School."* With the recent expansion of the FSU School of Medicine, the school was moved to Southwood.

Florida Highway Patrol Station If you learned to drive in Tallahassee in the 1950s thru 70s you went out to the Florida Highway Patrol station on Jacksonville Highway (US 90) to take your driving test. You would demonstrate your ability to parallel park, then drive through the neighborhood across the street being careful to use your blinkers and stop fully at all stop signs. A successful test would result in a brand-new license typed on a red stock paper.

Floridan Hotel opened May 2, 1927. It was said to have built out of 900,000 bricks. Located on the corner of Monroe and Call, it was one of Tallahassee's premier hotels. It boasted a large ballroom with crystal chandeliers, meeting rooms, dining room, and a porch with rocking chairs that ran across the front of the hotel. You could sit and watch people walk or drive by. Originally built three stories high with 68 rooms, an annex built in 1929 expanded its capacity to 150 rooms. In 1960's with the construction of hotels throughout the city, the hotel deteriorated and most of its customers were aging Tallahassee residents.

One such resident was Miss Ruby Diamond whom the Ruby Diamond Auditorium at FSU is named. She had lived there since 1927. She and others were forced to move in 1977 when the building was condemned. The building was demolished in July and August of 1985 and sat vacant until a parking lot was later built there. A new **Aloft** hotel is on the property today.

Floridan Hotel 1937

FM radio stations later became the norm in Tallahassee with most of the old AM stations converting over to FM. WBGM at 1213 West Tharp Street and WGLF were some of the first in town.

Florida Motor Court was located at 2325 Apalachee Parkway (Perry Highway) and had 44 units for rent.

Florida State College for Women became coed July 1, 1947 and was renamed **Florida State University**. Male students started as the Tallahassee Branch of the University of Florida in 1946 at Dale Mabry field.

Florida State started playing football in 1947 at Centennial Field. In 1950 they moved to Doak Campbell Stadium, capable of holding 15,000 fans. That year enrollment was over 6,000 students. The first game there was October 7, 1950, FSU beat Randolph Mason 40 to 7. In 1960-78 the stadium held 40,500. Service clubs worked the concessions. Scout's in uniform could sit in the wooden end zone bleachers for free, otherwise the cost was $1.00.

- **FSU's first golf course** was built around the stadium. It was a par three nine-hole golf course you could play using only a nine iron and a putter.
- **The Wescott building** constructed in 1911 is a center piece of the university located at the end of College Avenue on a spot formerly called **Gallows Hill**. It was destroyed in a fire in April of 1964 but was rebuilt.
- **College Avenue** was once called Clinton Street after Vice President George Clinton of the Jefferson and Madison administrations. The street name was changed in 1916 at the request of FSU President Dr. Edward Conradi to reflect something more associated with the school.
- **FSU Basketball games** were played at the Tully Gym, built in 1956. Before air conditioning the building was cooled by large fans and was one of the hottest buildings in town when it was crowded. A large steam whistle near the old Student Union used to wake Tallahassee workers up in the morning.

Florida Theater on North Monroe was one of two downtown theaters (the State Theater was the other.) They sat movie patrons in the main seating area as well as the upstairs balcony. A major event in Tallahassee was the night of March 26, 1960 when the theater burned down. Everyone had to drive by and gawk at the smoldering ruins. Luckily it was decided to rebuild the theater and it opened with high back seats and an improved concession stand. Lewis Spears was the General Manager.

The Florida Theater

Flowers Bakery Company at 1229 Gaines Street opened in 1937. They developed the blonde Little Miss Sunbeam trademark for their Sunbeam Bread products that were *"Batter Whipped with stronger texture and no holes."* They later moved their business to the home office in Thomasville. Their discount store is located on South Monroe today and still sells out dated goodies for a bargain.

Foremost Ice Cream store was located at 216 East Oakland Street. In the 1940's Foremost Dairy was located on Thomasville Road at Five Points near the entrance to Los Robles. Their name came from a famous Guernsey bull named Langwater Foremost. He was owned by the owner of J.C. Penny. The bull became the 4th most influential in the Guernsey line. Foremost Dairies was started in Jacksonville, Fl. Its motto was *"Better than Good, it's Foremost."*

Forsyth Memorial Hospital at 805 North Gadsden Street was Tallahassee's only hospital until Tallahassee Memorial was built. There had also been a field hospital at Dale Mabry that was operated until TMH was built. The building has also housed the Johnston Sanatorium and Edwards TB Hospital.

Fourth Avenue Supermarket (IGA) at 617 West Fourth Avenue served the Frenchtown community for years. It was run by the Millers.

Fountain Restaurant was located at 1921 West Tennessee Street and owned by Bruce Bishop. They offered upscale dining and a well-stocked bar.

Four Points was the name for the intersections of S. Monroe, Woodville Hwy, S. Adams, and Crawfordville Hwy. The intersection was regulated by stop signs. Tucker's Drive-In, George's Four Points and the Capital Drive-In Theater were there. All are gone now; the drive-in property is a holding pond. A gas station sits where the roads were reconfigured.

Fran's Dress Shoppe catered to Tallahassee's finest. They were located at 1801 Thomasville Road.

Fremac's was a men's clothing store located at 302 South Monroe Street.

French Town was the name given to the major black neighborhood of Tallahassee. Most lived there until the advent of the 1964 Civil Rights Bill that allowed them to move into formerly all-white neighborhoods. The area is bordered by West Seventh Avenue, Bronough Street, West Tennessee Street and Woodward Avenue. Macomb Street ran through the middle of the area and had many popular nightclubs such as the Red Bird and Café Deluxe. There were also pool halls, barber shops and restaurants there that did a thriving business. Today the area has changed. The Macomb area is filled with a City of Tallahassee government building and all the shops are gone.

Map of Historic Frenchtown

The Red Bird Café

Frisch's Big Boy Restaurant located on Tennessee Street. It was the home of the double-decker Big Boy sandwich. There was a plastic statue of the Big Boy with his stripped pants, paper hat, and a sling-shot hanging out of his pocket near the entrance. It later became a **Shoney's**. Today a **Chic-Fil-A** is at the location.

Frog Millhouse played sidekick to Gene Autry and Roy Rogers in their western movies when I was a kid. His real name was Smiley Burnett. In 1956 he came to Kate Sullivan Elementary School to entertain the kids and I got to meet him.

Frontier Shop at 1927 Thomasville Road was where you went to get your western gear.

Frosty Mack Tire Company at 1307 South Monroe was where you went to get tires in the forties and fifties.

Caroline Brevard School – Now the Bloxham Building

Garcia's Spanish Restaurant on Tennessee Street served the best black beans with onions and rice in town. It was owned by Sy CiCi. Today the building houses the **Cypress Restaurant**.

Garcia's Restaurant on Tennessee Street

Gayfer's was one of the anchor department stores for the Tallahassee Mall off of North Monroe Street. It was later bought by Dillard's.

Georges Four Points Liquor Store was run by the Petrandis family who owned Georges at Panacea. It was located at 3505 South Monroe at Four Points.

Gibbs French Shoppe was located at 118 South Monroe and offered the best in woman's apparel.

Gilberg's Fabric's was once located at 101-105 East Jefferson before moving to 123 South Monroe on the northeast corner of College and North Monroe. It later moved to the Northwood Mall. Long a store for the women of Tallahassee who like to sew, they advertised themselves as the *"House of 1,000 Fabrics."*

Good Time Charlie's was a place to get authentic Cajun food. You could get their swamp stew or red beans and rice just like it's supposed to be made. Located first at 1420 West Tennessee then at 2205 Apalachee Parkway it was owned by Charlie Newell. The Black Bean Café is located there now.

Governors Square Mall off the Apalachee Parkway opened Aug 16, 1979. The site was once a field used to land airplanes before Dale Mabry Field was opened.

Governor's mansion was originally built in 1906 at 700 South Adams. A new mansion was built in its place in 1955.

Gramlings Inc. was first opened in 1915 in the Old Union Bank building in the 100 block of S. Adams. In 1925 they built their current store at 1010 South Adams. Selling feed and seed to the locals, they closed their doors for good June 29, 2019 after 104 years in business.

Gramlings

Grand Prize Stamp Store was at 215 East Sixth Avenue.

Grant Furniture at 213 South Adams was a long-time furniture dealer in Tallahassee.

Green Derby on South Monroe near the railroad overpass was an early drive-in where you could also buy liquor even though Leon County was dry at the time (liquor sales prohibited).

Gridley Music Company was located at 111 West College Avenue and later 302 South Monroe.

The Governor Martin House built in 1934 was the residence of former Governor John W. Martin. The site is also the location of DeSoto's winter encampment in 1539. It's at 1001 Governor's Drive.

The Grove or the Call-Collins House was built by slaves of former Territorial Governor Richard Keith Call in 1840. It is now a museum.

The Grove

Heidi's in Setzer's Plaza   Lincoln High School on Brevard

Mom & Dad's on U.S. 27   Silver Sipper on S. Adams

Pisgah Church   Old Water Works on Gaines

H

Haunted House's there used to be a big house located on the site of the City of Tallahassee Utility office on Monroe Street. Thought to be haunted, it was abandoned for years. Another house, the Gladstone (known as White's Boarding House) at the intersection of N. Monroe and Thomasville Road was rumored (falsely) to be the site of a mass murder.

Hay's Grocery on Highway 27 was a mom and pop operation serving the northwest Tallahassee area around old Bainbridge Road. As a kid we used to go there to buy cigarettes that we would take back to the old barn on Hartsfield's Dairy and smoke.

Heidi's Bakery sold the best doughnuts and cream horns. Most wedding cakes in town were made at Heidi's for years. Originally located on Thomasville Road just after you merge from Calhoun it was next to a Lindy's Fried Chicken — the best of both worlds! A chiropractor is there now. Heidi's later moved to the Capital Plaza further down the road. It closed in June of 2009.

Hick's Drug Store was at 110 East Jefferson.

High Hat was a 1930s drive-in located at 1219 S. Monroe. You could also buy liquor there.

Hilton Hotel opened in 1970 where the old Tallahassee city hall was located on the corner of Park Avenue and Adams. It later became the Doubletree Hotel.

Hi-way Drive-In was located at 1900 North Monroe.

Holiday Inn Tallahassee had two Holiday Inn's. One at 1302 Apalachee Parkway and the *"Round"* Holiday Inn on West Tennessee Street. The Parkway Inn used to display congratulations and Happy Birthday messages. A CVS and Bank are at that location today. The Round Holiday Inn is now Sheraton Four Points

The Round Holiday Inn on Tennessee Street

Howard Johnson's on West Tennessee. We used to go there to get their 28 different flavors of ice cream. As kids we especially like the peppermint as it had pieces of candy in it. They were located in front of the Driftwood Motel and were also at 738 Apalachee Parkway just after the underpass.

Bill & Arvah Hopkins Bill was a tough-nosed State Attorney (1947-73) and Arvah a City Manager (1952-74) who was responsible for beautifying Tallahassee with rose gardens and dogwood trees.

Hokey Pokey If you attended Kate Sullivan School in the 1950's you will remember having Coach Wes Carter teaching your first-grade class the hokey pokey. *"You put your right foot in, you take your right foot out, you do the hokey pokey and you shake it all about."*

Holland's Restaurant at 106 E. Pensacola and 1002 North Monroe Street was a popular place to get good steaks and pies. They promised *"You'll never forget our melt in your mouth pies and rolls."* They also sold Kentucky Fried Chicken when the company first began selling franchises.

Homes many of the antebellum homes that marked old Tallahassee were built on Gadsden and Calhoun Streets. They had such names as Goodwood, the Brokaw/McDougal, the Knott House (built on East Park Ave & Calhoun Street in 1839-42), Randal-Lewis, Bowen, Bradford-Cobb, Rutgers, and Towle.

House of Pets was a pet store located on Tharpe Street. Other shops in the complex were the **House of Books, The Honey Tree, and Town & Country.** Before the stores were built the property was a sawmill. We used to play in the sawdust pile.

Hurricane Kate hit Tallahassee on Nov 21, 1985 just before Thanksgiving. Tallahassee's love affair with her big oaks and pines was suspended for a while as a chain saw became a necessity. Homes were crushed, roads were blocked, and electricity was out for weeks for some residents who held impromptu barbecues.

I

I-10 Interstate 10 opened 1972-3 in Leon County. Linking Jacksonville with Pensacola and points west to California it is officially known as the Christopher Columbus Transcontinental Highway. The Florida Transportation department lists it as State Road 8. It was originally scheduled to route through Tallahassee as an elevated expressway downtown to Gaines Street and be called the *"Seminole Expressway."* Opposition to the plan plus a donation of land from the developers of Killearn moved the route north of town. It changed the face of Leon County as well, allowing for easy access from those outlying areas to the city.

"Ice Cream Man" was what we called the man who drove a small white freezer truck around town selling ice cream treats. He had a set of bells on the top of his truck and would ring them as he slowly went down your street. Kids would run to beg their mothers for a dime to buy a *"Dilly"* or *"Nutty Buddy"* ice cream. He would stop his truck and open the freezer door on the side and pull out your treat. Every kid learned the times he would come in their neighborhood and would eagerly await his visits.

Icee's The cold frozen drinks were first sold at the Junior Stores in Tallahassee in the early 1960's. They offered grape, cola, and cherry. Another competitor soon developed was the **Ice Slushee**.

Industrial Savings Bank was located at 119 North Monroe.

J

J. Byron's was a department store located in the Tallahassee Mall.

J.M. Fields was the first megastore in Tallahassee. Built in 1963, you could buy groceries from the Food Fair Pantry Pride store next door without leaving the building. They also sold bakery goods, appliances, sporting goods, clothes, and automotive supplies all in one building. Located where the **Lake Ella Publix** is now, it was instrumental in overturning Tallahassee's blue laws that prohibited being open on Sundays.

Jr. Stores were another company that owned the convenience stores around town at one time.

Jerry's restaurants on North Monroe and on Tennessee Street were famous for their strawberry pies.

Jim & Milt's was built in the old Harrell's Grocery store that also housed a bait shop. It is located on Pensacola Street. Opened in 1968 by Jim Burgess & Milton Johnson. They hired the waiters from the Seven Steers to work there after that restaurant had burned down. Now run by Mike Flury & Sons, it is still in business today, offering delicious barbeque.

Jitney Jungle grocery stores were where people went to shop on the weekends. The first store was located on North Monroe where **Lucky Goat** and others are today. Mr. Kirby was the manager. The No. 2 store was located on West Tennessee where Momo's Pizza is today. The No. 3 store was on Lafayette Street. They also started the first convince stores in Tallahassee called **Jitney Juniors**.

Joe's Spaghetti House at 1713 Mahan Drive was run by Joe Graganella and his wife Anne. A popular meeting place for Legislators since the 1940's it was the scene of many brokered deals over good steaks or spaghetti.

64

Johnson's Sanatorium was the name of Tallahassee's only hospital in the early 1930's. It was located at 805 East Gadsden. Later it became the location of the W.T. Edwards T.B. Hospital before it moved out to Phillips Road. Forsyth Hospital was there in the 1960's. A design company is located there now.

Jones Brothers Hulon and Harvey were local racing legends. Hulon died at age 34 at the Valdosta Speedway. Harvey had a distinguished stock car career dominating the dirt tracks around the south.

Junior Museum was established in 1957. Originally located downtown, it opened in 1958 in the McMillan House on the NW coroner of W. Madison and S. Adams. Ten acres of land was purchased near Lake Bradford in 1960. The Big Bend Farm exhibit was built in 1961. In 1962 four new buildings were dedicated. More land was purchased in 1972. The Museum now consists of 52 acres. It will always be called the "Jr Museum" to old time Tallahassee folks even though the name was changed to the **Tallahassee Museum of History and Natural Science** in 1992.

K

Kelly's Casuals Ltd. was a woman's store located at 322 South Monroe Street.

Kennerly's Drugs at 1335 East Sixth Avenue was operated by Mr. Kennerly who would do magic tricks to cheer up sick children while their parents waited for their medicine.

A.M. Kidder & Co. Inc. Located in the Floridan Hotel building at 139 East Call, it was one of the few early brokerage firms in Tallahassee.

Killearn Estates opened in 1965 by J.T. William's and other investors, one being the late Mallory Horne. Because it was five miles from downtown it was considered so far out of town that people thought it was in Georgia. Most thought it too remote for any large scale development. The first home was built there in 1966.

Killearn Lakes Plantation was the second phase of the Killearn Properties development. The area first called itself a "private community" but later dropped it and shortened the name to Killearn Lakes.

Krispy Kreme doughnuts open at 1444 West Tennessee Street and Macomb bringing *"Hot Now"* melts in your mouth doughnuts to hungry drivers pulling into the store when the sign was lit. In January of 2002 the Tennessee Street store closed and a new one opened at 1300 East Park Avenue on the northeast corner of Magnolia and Park Avenue.

L

Lafayette Park Community Center opened November 5, 1957. It was where you went to dance after a Leon High School football game. Kids in junior high went to **Palmer Monroe Community Center** built in 1964 to dance at *"teen town."* Because the town was still segregated at the time, a center for blacks named **Dade Street Community Center** was opened in 1959.

Lake Ella is primarily a drainage pond today but it was a natural pond years ago. Originally called Bull Pond its name was changed in the 1930's. I remember as a kid going to the Lake Ella Fishathon's there. We also used to wade out to the island in the middle to steal duck eggs. The annual Fourth of July fireworks were held there until 1984. Today it has been made into a family spot where people go to walk their dogs and exercise by walking or running on the sidewalks around it.

Fishathon at Lake Ella

Lake Ella Motor Court at 1500 North Monroe consisted of 20 rock and brick cabins. It was also called the Tallahassee Auto Court at one time. Many of the old cabins now serve as businesss.

Lakes There are many lakes around Tallahassee. Some of the most well-known are: Lake Jackson, Lake Bradford, Miccosukee, Iamonia, Lafayette, and Hall.

Laura Bell Memorial Hospital at 316 East Virginia served the black population of Tallahassee in the early 1950's.

Lee's Grocery was a popular grocery in Tallahassee located on West Tennessee Street. The building later housed the Tallahassee Shelter.

Leon Federal Saving and Loan Association was located at 11 South Monroe. The front of the building was distinctive in the way their name was written across the building. A walk-up teller window was on the sidewalk outside.

Leon High School—Tallahassee's first high school opened on property between Park Avenue and Call Street in 1911. The three-story building was built by F.C. Gilmore who was also the architect that designed it. The building had four giant columns on the Park Avenue side as well as a sheet metal circular fire escape that was accessible from the second and third floors. After the high school moved to a new building on Tennessee Street it was used to house the Lewis M. Lively Technical Center. It was demolished in 1960's. The Leroy Collins Public Library is now located there.

"Old "Leon High School

"**New**" **Leon High School** was built with depression area WPA monies. It opened May 28, 1937. Its present location is on Tennessee Street. Prior to construction of the school the area in front of the building used today as an athletic field was a pond.

"New" Leon High School

Leon's Bobby Benson Field was named after a former student/athlete who died of pneumonia in 1938. The concrete seating for the field, completed in 1939, could accommodate 840 people.

Leon's "Old" Gym was built in 1949. Prior to its construction the basketball team played their games at the Armory on North Monroe and Seventh Ave.

Leon's "New" Gym was built in 1967.

Leon County Public Library was first housed in the Columns at Park and Adams next to the old Union Bank. It opened March 21, 1956. In need of more space it was moved to the former Elks Lodge Building on Monroe Street in 1962. In May of 1978 the library moved again to the basement of the Northwood Mall. The library finally found permanent residence on Call Street in 1991. In September of 1993 the building was rededicated in memory of Governor LeRoy Collins.

Leon County Court House was built in 1828 on the north side of Park Avenue between Monroe and Adams. It later moved to Jefferson and Monroe Street.

Leon County Armory *"the old armory,"* located at 1400 North Monroe on the corner of Monroe and Seventh Avenue. It was built in 1935 to house National Guard Company M by the WPA with New Deal money. Besides being a armory it was used by Leon High for basketball games until 1949 when they built their own gym on campus. The Tallahassee Parks and Recreation department also used its wooden floors for roller skating and youth basketball games.

The Tallahassee Tumbling Tots practiced there from 1949 to 1972. In 1978 the National Guard moved to a new armory on Capital Circle and the building was converted into the **Tallahassee Senior Center**.

Leon Theater on West Tennessee Street was owned by the Stone family and for years served the black community of Frenchtown. It was later renamed Randy's Campus Art Theater and showed adult movies.

The Leon Theater

Lerner's was a woman's dress shop on the Apalachee Parkway.

Lewis State Bank at 215 South Monroe Street is one of Florida's oldest banks, begun in 1856.

Radical Jack Lieberman was a colorful and outspoken student at Florida State University in the 1960's. At a time when political unrest against the Vietnam War hit the college campuses, Radical Jack was a leader of the demonstrators.

Lincoln Drive- In Theater was located on Pasco Street.

Lincoln High School opened in 1876 was originally located on Brevard Street. For years it served as the only school for black students. Classes were for grades 1-12. It later became a high school for black students before integration in the 1960's. Their mascot was a tiger. Named after Abraham Lincoln, Frank Nims was principal. It was closed in 1969. Another Lincoln High School was opened 1975-6 in northeast Tallahassee near the Federal Correction Institute and serves all races. Their mascot is a Trojan soldier.

Linden's Children' Shop was a store specializing in children's clothes at 120 South Monroe.

Lindy's Fried Chicken owned by Ray Salis, Jr. sells the best chicken sandwich in town. They have been in business since the 1960's and used to have a store on Thomasville Road next door to Heidi's Bakery.

Lillian's was a woman's dress shop located at 204 South Adams owned by "Ms. Lillian "Cox.

Lichgate on High Road was built by FSU Professor Laura Jensen. The word means "corpse" and in olden days bodies would be placed there until the funeral.

Little Brother was a neat store to find unique gifts, *Jellybelly* jellybeans, and old- time candy. Located at 206 East Sixth Avenue they sold gifts, pewter, cards and imported goods. The **Grey Fox** had occupied the building on the corner of North Monroe and Sixth Avenue but recently closed. **Voncelles**, a wedding gown store is there now.

Little Folks Store at 133 North Monroe was operated by the Finley's. If you were having a birthday or going to one, you would shop at Little Folks for great toys. They sold bow & arrow sets, super balls, squirt rings, wet-me dolls and baseball gloves. They later followed the store migration from the city and moved out to the Steinmart Shopping Center off Thomasville Road before closing their doors.

Lively Corner was the name for the area around the Lively Drug Store on the corner of Clinton (College) and Monroe in the 1860's. The drug store had the first soda fountain in town. Named for the bars and gambling that went on in the area it was probably a sight to see. The corner later became the location for Bennett's Drug Store in 1937.

Lively Vocational School (now Lively Technical School) It was started in 1937 by Mr. Lewis M. Lively, a local businessman. It was originally at the old Leon High School building on Duval and Park. The school opened with one full-time and one half-time instructor and 52 students. It now has two campus's, the main one at 500 Appleyard Drive, and another at the Tallahassee Regional Airport.

Los Robles is Spanish for *"The Oaks."* It was Tallahassee's first platted neighborhood and suburb. Developed in the 1920's by Leon F. Lonnbaldh and A.E. Thornton, the city limits were at its gates. The gates were built in 1926 and due to damages were remodeled in 2004. The subdivision has 110 homes. The Burch Apartments on Cristobal Drive were owned by my grandparents Harry and Margaret Burch. In 1937 they contracted with Claude A. Pichard to build theirs and another for my great aunt Lillian Marrow. My grandfather used to tell my mother that "someday the city limits of Tallahassee would come out as far as the gates of Los Robles." I remember as a child climbing over the top of the entrance gate.

Gates at Los Robles

Loopers Subs located at 1395 E. Lafayette St. was a Tallahassee favorite. A **Vertigo Burgers & Fries** is now located in the old building.

LUM's selling hotdogs cooked in beer with a cold pitcher of brew was a sure draw for college students and beer drinkers everywhere. Tallahassee had two locations, one on West Tennessee Street and the other on the Parkway in the late 1960's and 70's.

M

Mae's was a woman's clothing store located at 115 North Calhoun Street.

Mahan Drive in 1935 Fred Mahan's Monticello Nursery donated 35,000 to 40,000 plants to beautify the 25-mile stretch of Highway 90 between Tallahassee and Monticello. Mainly crepe myrtles, they were planted over a period of eight years. In 1953 the highway was officially named the Fred Mahan Drive.

Mahalia Jackson's was a restaurant on South Adams by FAMU named for the singer. It specialized in the best fried chicken and fried biscuits you ever ate. When they closed, they were missed by many.

Majik Markets were another company name for the local convenience stores in Tallahassee.

Mangel's at 112 South Monroe Street offered a wide range of woman's clothing.

Masonic Building for Jackson Lodge #1, Florida's oldest Masonic Lodge used to be at the corner of Adams and College. It is now the **Governor's Club**. The lodge moved out the Parkway to a new building.

Manny's was a popular restaurant to go eat good food and meet friends for coffee and small talk. Originally in the old **Tallahassee Motor Court Restaurant,** they later moved to the Lake Ella Shopping Center.

Maxie Burgers was a successful hamburger store that served hamburgers and tasty French fries fresh, hot and in a hurry. Their small two-sided drive up windows allowed customers to get their orders quickly. They later sold out to **Rally Burgers**.

May Day was always celebrated with a parade downtown. The May Queen & Court tradition ran from 1833 to1974. The Queen and her court were chosen by Leon High students. The day was celebrated with pretty girls on floats, marching bands and the Maypole dance. With the integration of the public schools, the thought of celebrating antebellum Tallahassee and pre-emancipation times did not sit well. The school stopped choosing a court and it fell to the Springtime Tallahassee organizers but was finally discontinued. Later the old May Oak was cut down due to disease. The stump is all that remains.

May's Electric was located at 118 East Park Avenue. They later merged with Monroe's Appliances.

Mays-Monroe has been selling appliances in Tallahassee for years. Ray Monroe and his wife star in their own corny commercials and they used to remind people that *"The Round Holiday Inn is next to us,"* before they later moved to Capital Circle.

McCrory's was a five and dime department store located at 216-20 South Monroe. They had their merchandise displayed in bins and also had a food counter. The store closed in 1975.

McDonalds Tallahassee's first McDonalds was built in the early 1960's at 1701 East Tennessee Street. Hamburgers were 15 cents and cheeseburgers were 25 cents. Before Ronald McDonald came about in 1966 there was a character that looked like a hamburger wearing a chef's hat on the McDonalds sign. Their sign also advertised the number of hamburgers they had sold. The building was easily recognized by its red and white tiles and yellow arches.   It became a popular teen hang-out where you would cruise through the parking lot looking to see who was there. Early advertisements called it *"the drive in with the arches,"* and advertised *"tasty food--thrifty prices."* A What-A-Burger now stands in its place on Tennessee Street.

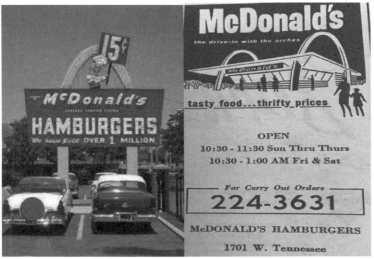

Mecca Restaurant a favorite for FSU students was located at 111 South Copeland in the middle of the block. **Bill's Bookstore** was later built in its place. **The Amber House**, another favorite was on the corner.

Mendelson's Department Store was owned and run by Sidney and Harold Mendelson. Before it was called Mendelson's it was known as the Surprise Store. With free gift wrap and home delivery, they also had the only escalator in town. Children would ride upstairs to see Santa Claus at Christmas time. The original store was founded by their father Sam in 1912 on the corner of Jefferson and Adams. It moved to 105 South Monroe at the southeast corner of Park and Monroe in the 1950's. A fire in 1967 closed them temporarily but then they moved south up and across Monroe street to a location near Wilson's department store. With the opening of the Northwood Mall they moved with other downtown merchants to the new Mall in 1969. They sold their business in 1973.

Mendelson's on N. Monroe Street

Mike's Texaco and Beer Barn at 556 West Tennessee was the place to rent a keg of beer or just buy a six pack. They also had a car wash and filling station. The place was recently sold but still bears the name Mike's after the new owner.

Mill Bakery was located off of North Monroe. It became a family tradition to go to the Mill to buy their fantastic large muffins after church on Sunday.

Millers Landing is a boat ramp on Lake Jackson. To get to it you have to go out Meridian Road. It is located beside the Forest Meadows Tennis Courts. We used to go down the red clay road to fish out of the landing and in later years' kids would meet there on the weekends to have drinking parties.

Millers Bootery was a woman's shoe shop on Monroe Street.

Miniature Train in the 1950's a Mr. McHarry ran a miniature train over tracks he had laid on his property off Highway 90 at Highland Drive. School children would come to picnic and ride the train.

Moby Dicks on Thomasville Road in Bradfordville. A great seafood restaurant specializing in fried catfish. They had a pond next to the restaurant where you could go feed the catfish your left-over hushpuppies. The pond would boil as the catfish swarmed to eat the food, not realizing they were being fattened up to be food themselves. A **Target Store** now stands on the property.

Mom & Dad's was located at 4175 Apalachee Parkway from 1963 to 2017. Long a favorite among Tallahassee diners and legislators, they served great food. Specializing in homemade pasta and sauces, they also made killer steaks. The family sold the business in 2014 but the great Italian recipes were retained by the new owners. They moved the business to a shopping center on Bannerman Road.

The Moon Scott Carswell opened it April 2, 1985 in the old A&P store on Lafayette Street. Offering concerts by famous musicians, it has been an integral part of the music scene in Tallahassee.

Moon's Jewelers was originally located at 536 College. In 1959 they moved to 536 North Monroe. The owner, Lester Moon, handled their television and radio commercials and coined a popular phrase telling buyers *"If you don't know your diamonds, be sure you know your jeweler."*

Morrison's Sunday buffet used to be where everyone in Tallahassee would go for Sunday dinner. It was located on the corner of Pensacola and South Adams Streets. It later moved into the Tallahassee Mall. The food line always started with the desserts and every kid had to get the best piece of pie or cake, or favorite flavor of pudding or Jell-O. At the end of the line was the man carving the prime roast beef. Waiters would carry your tray to the table and discreetly wait for a tip.

Serving line at Morrisons

Mug's and Movies was a movie theater where you could watch a movie and eat a meal. It was located in the old **Varsity Theater** building at the intersection of High Road and West Tennessee Street. Another was located in the Timberlane Shops off Timberlane Road.

Mutt & Jeff's was a popular hangout for kids. Selling hamburgers (called a Wimpy), fries, onion rings, slaw dogs and special named drinks like a Coke or Root Beer float (Black Cow), Cherry Smash, or a Cherry Vanilla Lemonade called an *"Ickey."* It was located at Five Points outside the gates to Los Robles. The interior had a small counter, two booths, two tables, two bathrooms and a place for a pinball machine you could play for a nickel. It opened in March of 1948 and was operated by Arthur Pichard (Mutt) and DeWitt Trawick (Jeff). You could drive up to the service window on the side of the building or wait in the parking lot for a car-hop to take your order. Mutt & Jeff's closed in 1981 when they decided to retire. The property was sold to local developer Bill Childers. In 1984 he sold it to Fincher Smith who opened the **Coconut Cowboy,** then renamed it the **Paradise Grill**. **Midtown Caboose** is there today.

- **Before Mutt & Jeff's**--In 1935 before it was leased by Pichard and Trawick the business had been called **Blue Heaven** and was run by the Veal brothers from Moultrie, Georgia. Operated as a take-out restaurant only, they sold hamburgers, sandwiches and beer.
- Prior to being called **Blue Heaven** it had been known as the **Little Dipper.** It had been built to look like the Little Dipper and opened in 1931 or 32. It was a drive-in operated by Arthur Collins, former Governor Leroy Collins brother. The building burned and was rebuilt and named Blue Heaven.
- Prior to the **Little Dipper** the place was a juice bar and landscape business called the **Nectar Garden** that opened in 1927.
- From 1927 to 1981 it was Tallahassee's oldest continuously operated drive-in.

Mutt and Jeff's

The Little Dipper

Muzz's Place was a beer joint with a pool table that catered to blacks. Located in Bradfordville it was also a place many white underage high school students went to buy beer. I remember riding on the back of a Honda 150 way out Meridian Road to Muzz's to buy beer in the late 1960's.

N

National Shirt Shops was located at 122 South Monroe Street and offered a variety of shirts and other clothing for the well-dressed man.

Looking west at College and Monroe Streets

Nick's Café opened in 1955, is Tallahassee's oldest café still in business. It is located at 1431 South Monroe next to the former Terry Rosa Hardware store at 1429 South Monroe.

Nic's Toggery opened at 322 South Monroe on the east side of Monroe. They later moved south to other side of Monroe by the courthouse (across from Lewis state bank.) It is one of downtown Tallahassee's original stores predating the malls.

Neisner's department stores were located at 1155 Apalachee Parkway and 1950 West Tennessee Street. They sold the usual five and dime goods you would expect for a department store.

Nellie's Dress Shop was located at 104 ½ South Monroe.

Noble Romans was a family pizza restaurant located in the Public shopping center at 1-10 and Thomasville Road. The offered a great deep-dish pizza.

Northwood Mall opened in 1969 and except for the Publix store, Eckerd's Drugs and Rheinauers, all the stores were locally owned. Original stores were Millers, Mendelson's, Gilberg's, and Turners. Others in the mall were Crystal Connection, Seminole Barber Shop (run by Coach who knew how to give a buzz cut), Maas Brothers, Olan Mills, Elaine Powers, Walden Books, and Dubey's Book Store.
Downstairs was the Division of Drivers License's, Silver Slipper, Tallahassee Parks and Recreation Department, Orange Julius, Leon County Public Library, Theaters.

Notable School Teachers/Administrators:
- **Kate Sullivan** called "Miss Kate," she taught for 47 years. **Kate Sullivan School** was dedicated on December 1948 and became Leon counties third elementary school. Mrs. Pope taught first grade. Sara Belcher taught third grade and was later Principal. Wes Carter was the "Coach," and Mrs. Wooten taught music.

- **Augusta Raa** was an educator. **Augusta Raa Jr. High** opened in 1959. M.O. Harrison, Principal Mr. Hilaman, Assistant Principal, Gene Raker and Jerry Steiger were coaches, Miss Carolyn Glenn was the choral director and wrote the Alma Mater for the school. Mr. Bradford was band director.
- **Leon High School**: Mr. Ashmore, Principal, Mike Conley, Assistant Principal, Romulus Thompson started the Leon Band, he was followed by Oliver Hobbs.
- **Lincoln High School:** Frank Nims was its principal. Nims Elementary is named for him.
- **Carolyn Brevard** was a teacher at Leon and an FSU History professor.
- **Amos P. Godby** was the Leon County School superintendent.
- **Francis (Frank) Hartsfield Sr.** was an educator and former School Superintendent.
- **Dorothy Holmes** was the Negro School Supervisor in segregated Tallahassee.
- **Lillian Ruediger** was an educator and the White School Supervisor in segregated Tallahassee.
- **James S. Rickards** was an educator and Ex. Secretary of the Fla Education Association.
- **Sealy Elementary** was named after Romero Mitchel Sealy a former State Supervisor of Secondary Education from 1922-27.
- **Leonard A. Wesson** was a former Mayor of Tallahassee.

Notables who have visited Tallahassee:
- **Billy Graham** held a revival at the Civic Center.
- **George Wallace** came to the North Florida Christian School for a rally during his 1968 Presidential run.

- Richard Nixon visited the city airport in 1970

COME AND GREET
The President of the United States

RICHARD NIXON

TALLAHASSEE MUNICIPAL AIRPORT
Main Terminal

2:00 P.M.
Wednesday October 28, 1970
Ample Parking Entertainment

- The Duke of Windsor
- William Jennings Bryant spoke at the old Leon High School on Feb 29, 1916 against alcohol.

O

Oak Valley Golf course at 555 Ocala Road was built on property surrounding the home of local attorney Clyde Atkinson. It soon went out of business. The property today is the site for Heritage Grove and the new Florida State Fraternity Row off of Ocala Road.

The Oasis 119 West Jefferson.

Ocala Road was cut through from Tharpe Street to Tennessee Street in the late 1960's. Many thought the road might be named Low Road since the road running parallel to it on the east was High Road.

Old South Drive-In was located at 1620 South Monroe in the 1950's and later moved to 1706 North Monroe. They sold shrimp, oysters and chicken in a box to go. They also offered barbeque sandwiches.

Orange Balls made of Styrofoam were given away as a promotional gimmick for a radio station in the 1960's and became the *"in"* thing to put on your antenna. People thought they would help located your car in the parking lot but it was kind of hard to do when everyone else had one on their car as well.

P

Palmer Monroe Community Center hosted weekly dances called *Teen Town.*

Parks in old Tallahassee were limited. The oldest established parks were Myers, Levy, Lafayette, and Winthrop.

Parkway Bowl was at 1230 Apalachee Parkway. A business office is now in the building, located behind the Walgreens on Magnolia and the Parkway.

Pasquales Pizza was a college town favorite.

Pearle Vision Center located in Thomasville, Georgia supplied glasses and contact lens to local residents. We heard about them through WCTV Channel Six.

J.C. Penny's was located at 128 North Monroe next to the Woolworths department store and the Florida Theater. Today a federal courthouse takes up most of the block. As a kid we would go there to buy school clothes. They later moved to the Governors Square Mall.

Peppermint Patio was a juke joint frequented by the local black population. It was located at 138 Canal Street close to the Florida A & M campus.

Pepsi-Cola Bottling Company at 311 E. Jennings also bottled Sun Crest drinks.

Perry Highway was the name for U.S. 27 going out of Tallahassee. Because it went to the city Perry it was called the Perry Highway.

Perry Highway Outdoor Theater was one of two outdoor theaters in Tallahassee that opened in the 1950's (the other was the Capitol). It had one screen and the lot held about 300 cars. It was located on the northwest corner of the Capital Circle and the Perry Highway (US 27). A Days Inn motel is on the property today. It went out of business in the1970's.

Perry Highway Drive-In

Phone Numbers If you lived in Tallahassee in the 1950's you probably remember when the phone numbers were only five digits, mine was 2-9742. In 1961 as a sign of the times, all phone numbers increased to seven numbers. There were only four prefixes available depending on where you lived- 222, 223, 224 or 385.

Pic & Save was a drug store in the Capital or Setzer's Plaza at 1836 Thomasville Road.

Piggly Wiggly grocery was located at 607 North Adams.

Pikes Studio was where you went to get quality family and individual portrait pictures. They were located at 107 West College.

Pisgah United Methodist Church was organized in 1830. The building on the property off Pisgah Road was built in 1859. The cemetery on the church grounds is still in service today, as is the church.

Playing around old Tallahassee neighborhoods used to consist of sliding down the drainage ditches when it rained and afterwards walking on the hot steaming streets on July afternoons. We used to go out at night when the "bug spray man" drove his truck through the neighborhood and run behind his truck in the clouds of spray, never knowing anything about how it could hurt you. We would play freeze tag in car headlights, jumping in the ditch before the lights came down the road.

Population of Tallahassee/Leon County has steadily grown through the years. It was a small place until the 1990s. In the 1920s the entire county had 18,000 people, 1930- 23,000, 1940- 30,000, 1950- 51,000, 1960- 75,000, 1970-100,000, 1980-150,000.

Prime Meridian for the State of Florida is located near the **Cascade's Park**, its coordinates are N 30 26.069, W 084 16.626. It is from this point that all property line surveys in the State of Florida were begun.

Proctor & Proctor at 215 North Monroe was Tallahassee's Cadillac dealer. Though they have moved around town since the 1940's, they are still in business today.

Post Office in federal court building on Park Avenue.

Purple Poodle was a store offering fine linens and bath necessities located at 1203 Thomasville Road.

Putnam Jewelers at 308 South Monroe was a long time Tallahassee Jeweler.

Putt-Putt golf located behind the Tallahassee Mall entertained many kids and teenage dates.

Q

Quaker House was a restaurant specializing in fried chicken. They also served Duchess Ice Cream. We would go there to get the double-decker cones. It was located at 1425 West Tennessee Street on the corner of Bryan Street. Today Bryan Street has been reconfigured, a Papa John's Pizza store is on the site.

Quincy's Family Steakhouse served affordable steak dinners with great yeast rolls. They were located off of Timberlane Road. Many times we would go there just to order a dozen hot rolls to go.

Quality Cleaners on College and Duval was in business at that location for many years. In the 1960's Jerry Ingram, a Tallahassee boy was killed in the Vietnam War. He had always said he liked the painting they had on the side of the cleaners that read *"Isn't it great to live in Tallahassee."* The owners had it touched up and dedicated to his memory.

In memory of Jerry Ingram

R

Randy's Campus Art Theater was located in the old Leon Theater on West Tennessee Street. They featured *"adult"* movies. It was later closed and the property was converted to the Tallahassee Rescue Mission for the homeless.

Randy's Campus Art Theater

Rainey Cawthon's was a Goodyear Tires dealer located on the corner of North Monroe and Brevard Street.

Rally Burgers bought out the Maxie's franchise and has stores on Monroe, Apalachee Pkwy & Hwy 90.

Rax roast beef sold *"killer"* roast beef sandwiches. They were located at 2511 Apalachee Parkway.

Red Bird Café was a popular nightspot in Frenchtown located at 405 North Macomb Street.

Red & Sam's Fish camp on Lake Jackson was run by Red Smith and Sam Crowder. A popular boat launch area, fishermen could get their picture in the paper by their sign that read *"Caught at Red & Sam's."* They introduced an automatic fish scaling machine in the 1960's that looked like a large dryer tub that would spin the fish and scale them. Once located on the north side of the lake, it later moved to the south side.

Record Stores like records in Tallahassee, have come and gone. The oldest were **Nelsons** and **Gridley's**, later there was **Turtles**, **Peaches**, and **Vinyl Fever**.

Red & White Store was on Miccosukee Road past the hospital.

Rheaburg's Grocery at Bradfordville was a mom and pop operation suppling groceries to the Bradfordville area before Killearn Lakes was built. After the **Sing Store** was built on Bannerman in the 1980's they sold out to a nursery that later closed. A Target Store sits on the property today.

Rheinauers was an upscale department store located in the Northwood Mall. It was one of the original stores when the mall opened.

Rhoden Cove Landing was named after Mr. Lloyd Rhoden, former North Florida Fair Manager and Leon County Extension Director. Located off of Meridian Road, the landing is on Lake Jackson. Kids used the dead-end area to meet and have drinking parties there for years.

Rhodes Furniture sold high end furniture and was located at 1122 Thomasville Road on the corner of Fifth Avenue. Today the old store has been converted to the shops at Midtown.

Richard's Leather at 103 East College was always fun to walk in and smell the rich smell of leather. They sold a variety of leather goods and luggage and later moved to the Governor's Square Mall.

Ritz Theater was one of the earlier theaters in Tallahassee located at 108 South Monroe.

Robbin's Sam Robbin's Department Store was located at 115 East Jefferson.

Rocky's was a popular bar and nightspot for Tallahassee locals out on the town. It was located on the southeast corner of Allen Road and North Monroe at the Tallahassee Mall.

Ron Galimore's Gym was opened by Olympic gymnast Ron Galimore near 1-10 and Thomasville Road. The first Afro-American gymnast, he was supposed to compete in the 1980 Olympics but was unable when the U.S. boycotted them.

Rose Bowery selling women's shoes was at 111 East College.

Rose Printing Co. is owned by the Rosenberg family. Longtime printers and publishers they are located off of Appleyard Drive.

Roundup Drive-In at 1825 Thomasville Road.

Royal Burger Drive-In at Dewey and West Tennessee street.

Royal Crown-Nehi Bottling Company was located at 210 East Oakland Avenue. School kids used to come to the plant on field trips and after watching the bottling process would get a free drink.

SAE Lion was a statue at the Sigma Alpha Epsilon house at FSU. The fraternity house's statue located on West Tennessee Street was often the target of vandals who would paint the lion. Rumor had it if you were caught by the fraternity brothers, they would shave your head before letting you go.

San Can Drive-In was located at 1825 Thomasville Road. It was named for the owners two daughters.

Sawyer & Son sold and repaired lawn mowers at 425 East Tennessee Street.

Sears & Roebuck was located at 311 South Monroe on corner of Pensacola and Monroe in the 1950's. The spot is where the Leon County Courthouse stands today. In 1958 they moved out the Parkway to 1233 Apalachee Parkway. The plaza became known as the Sears shopping plaza. Today the plaza holds a **Ross** store and the **New Leaf Market** to name a few. Sears moved into the Governor's Square Mall when it opened and is still there today.

Sealy Elementary School was named after Romero Mitchel Sealy a former State Supervisor of Secondary Education from 1922-27. The original school was located where today's Tallahassee Police Department is at 234 East Seventh Avenue then called Capital Boulevard. Tallahassee's second elementary school, they started the first school lunch program on a concession basis in 1932. The school was moved to its present location at 2815 Allen Road behind the Tallahassee Mall in 1970.

Seminole Truck Stop and Diner was a popular eating spot out on West Tennessee Street long before the area was built up.

Setzer's Grocery was located on Thomasville Road in what became Capital Plaza but was once called simply *"Setzer's."*

Seven Sea's Restaurant was located next to the Capital at 318 South Monroe.

Seven Steers at 1817 West Tennessee Street was the best places to buy a hamburger in Tallahassee in the early 1960's. Their hamburgers were named Wrangler and Maverick, etc. each with a different sauce, all flame broiled. The car hops were black gentlemen who would climb the stairs to the hill above the restaurant where cars would park and flash their lights for service. The store was closed due to a fire. The owners reopened as Jim & Milts on Pensacola with the carhops now serving as waiters, but that soon stopped as they could not make enough money waiting tables. **Guthrie's Chicken** is there now.

Seven-Up Bottling Company was located at 308 East Palmer Street.

S&H green stamps were prized in the 1960's and 70's. Groceries and gas stations offered the stamps with a $1.00 purchase equaling 10 stamps. There were 50 stamps to a page and when you filled your book it could be redeemed for gifts like kid's toys, toasters or a lamp. Families would gather around the dinner table and fill their books, usually with the kids doing the licking! A gift catalogue was available to determine how many books equaled what you wanted. A trading store where you could redeem your books of stamps was located at 1545 South Monroe Street. Another trading stamp company was the **Plaid Stamp** store at 739 North Monroe.

Shaw's Furniture on corner of College and Duval was a Tallahassee institution.

Shingles Chicken House sold the best fried chicken in town. Located at 905 Miles Street, the Harry Shingles family ran the business for years until it closed in 2008. Doing a strictly cash only business you would place your order and sit at a table to wait for your order to be cooked. Prior to owning the business Harry Shingles ran it as the Chicken House.

Skyline Motor Lodge and Lounge at 2301 West Tennessee was a popular nightspot for locals in the 1970's. The lounge later burned down and the motel was demolished to make room for a car lot.

Shells Oyster Bar was originally located in a gas station and had five stools. It is now located behind the original store and Maners Garage.

Sid's Four Points lounge was a good place to have a drink and also to get in trouble if you were not careful. Located near the Capital Drive-In it was a popular night spot for years.

Sinclair Dinosaurs used to stand in front of the Sinclair gas stations. One remains in front of a house off of Highway 90 near the Pat Thomas Law Enforcement Training Center.

Silver Lake off of Highway 20 was where your parents sent you to camp in the summer to get a break. Kids would stay in cabins and swim in the lake. Always maintaining to a "buddy system' you had to be able to grab their hand and hold it in the air whenever they blew their whistle and asked you to show your buddy.

Silver Slipper called itself *"Tallahassee's Most Exclusive Dining Room"* for 71 years. The restaurant catered to the rich and powerful in Tallahassee and state government. Their private booths were the scene of many backroom deals between legislators and lobbyists. Originally located on Perkins Street between Monroe and Adams, they moved to the Northwood Mall when the downtown businesses started their flight. It later moved to Scotty Lane near the Tallahassee Mall (the road was later renamed Silver Slipper Lane). The business closed its doors for good in April of 2009 after the Leon High class of 1969 celebrated their 40th reunion there, and with it a piece of old time Tallahassee disappeared forever.

Silverstein's Bakery on Monroe near Seventh Avenue was a place where you went in the 1930's to get bakery goods.

Sims Murders changed Tallahassee's laid-back way of life. October 22, 1966. Dr. Robert W. Sims, his wife Helen and 12-year-old daughter Joy are murdered in their home off Gibbs Drive. Rumors flew as to who was the culprit. The Stiles pond behind their house was drained looking for the murder weapon. No weapons were ever found or a suspect arrested. The case is still open today. That night Tallahassee lost her innocence. People rushed to put locks on their doors and buy handguns for protection. The simple small-town life was gone forever.

Sinks are caused by cave-ins of limestone shelfs; Leon County is home to many sinks. Some of the most well-known are Blue, Cherokee, Big & Little Dismal, Horn Springs, River, and Gopher sinks.

Sizzler Steak House offered good steaks at an affordable price and was frequented by young families. They had two locations, one on North Monroe which is now **Old Time Buffet** and another on West Tennessee Street that is now a charter school.

Sing stores and Suwannee Swifty were the names of local convenience stores in town through the years.

Smokey Hollow was the name given to the community that used to inhabit the area where the Department of Transportation, Florida Fish and Wildlife and Apalachee Parkway underpass now stand. Rough borders of the area were E. Lafayette St., the CSX RR tracks, Myers Park and Myers Park Lane. A poor black community, it was made up of wooden shacks. Their smoking chimneys in the wintertime and the location gave rise to the name Smokey Hollow. While it was home to many it was also an embarrassment to others in the fact that it was located almost at the front doors of the state capitol. When the Apalachee Parkway was built in 1957 it cut the community in half and was the beginning of the end for the residents. All that remains today are a few houses behind the DOT building.

Snow is not a common thing in Tallahassee so when it happens everyone goes a little crazy over it—which those who were used to it in the north could never understand. Three inches fell on Tallahassee Feb 13, 1958 and everyone went out to play in the snow and make snowmen, some for the first and only time in their lives. As luck would have it, I had pneumonia at the time and was not able to play outside, but I did get to throw a snowball my mother made for me when she carried me to the door to look at the snow in the yard. I remember listening to the radio station broadcasting from the Dixieland Drive-In when it started snowing and they had a snowman building contest on the hoods of the patron's cars. Tallahassee would see another light dusting of snow in Feb of 1973. On December 23, 1989 one inch fell right before Christmas and Tallahassee had its first white Christmas.

Snow Cones were always available from the man in the Sno-Cone truck at all the local ball games.

Southernaire Motel at the intersection of Brevard Street and West Tennessee Street was owned by Clyde Atkinson a local attorney and entrepreneur. The motel was torn down in 2009 and an apartment complex the **Grand Marc** at Tallahassee is there today.

Spartan Restaurant was located at 415 North Monroe. It opened in 1969. Because of its good food and close proximity to the capitol it was frequented by locals and state legislators on a regular basis.

Springtime Tallahassee began March 23, 1968 the brainchild of Betty McCord. Fear that the legislators who were in the process of reapportionment might move the capital to a site more central to the state was one of the reasons for starting the annual celebration to show off Tallahassee's history and charm. I drove one of the convertibles carrying a Honey Queen from Georgia in the first parade.

Stafford's Jeweler's at 313 South Adams and later at 106 South Monroe had a big diamond on their sign. They later opened a store in the Northwood Mall.

State Bakery & Pastry Shop was located at 324 South Adams and run by Dennis Willet. It first opened for business in 1918. State employees would stop for coffee and doughnuts in the mornings. The business is gone today.

State Theater was located at 108 East College on north side of College between Adams and Monroe Street. It was called Daffin's Theater in the 1920's and was the only air-conditioned building in Tallahassee in the 1930s. It was torn down in 1988 to make way for the **High Point Center** which now occupies the location.

Strickland's Shoe Store or the Buster Brown Store was located at 115 E. College. They sold Buster Brown shoes *"the shoe with the boy and the dog inside"* was owned and operated by Roy Strickland.

Street Names in Tallahassee were first modeled after the states where her first settlers came from like Virginia, Georgia, Carolina and Tennessee. Prominent citizens in National and Florida history were also recognized Jefferson, Madison, Adams, Monroe, Duval, Gadsden, Calhoun, and Call. The city was laid out symmetrically with a Capitol square at the center and four other squares. The first lots in the city were sold in April of 1825, the city was incorporated December 9, 1825.

Other street name origins were:

- **Blair Stone** was named after man who was head of the Centel telephone company, other streets named after its employees were Mayhew, Greer, Armstrong, Gearhart & McKee.
- **Monroe Street** was named after James Monroe when he was President in 1823.
- **College Avenue** was originally named Clinton Street after Vice President George Clinton who served under Thomas Jefferson and James Madison but was changed in 1912 at the request of FSU president Edward Conradi.
- **Adams Street** was named after Sec of State John Quincy Adams in 1823.
- **Park Avenue** was formerly named McCarthy street and 200 Foot Street.
- **Lively corner** was the name for the property owned by the Lively's on the corner of College Avenue and Monroe Street where Bennett's Drug Store was.
- **McCord Point** was the name for the intersection of Monroe and Thomasville Road an old standard Oil station was located there.

Steyermans Style Shop was at 108 N. Monroe.

Stores in Tallahassee used to be closed on Sundays, open 1/2-day Saturday, and closed all-day Wednesday.

Storkette was a store to buy items for infants located at 103 South Monroe Street.

Rod Sterling came to Tallahassee in 1962 and he visited Ruediger Elementary. He came walking down the school breezeway escorted by some teachers. I got to shake hands with him and swore I would never wash that hand again.

Streaking supposedly got its start at Florida State University. In 1974, 200 streaker's staged a streak-in down Tennessee Street- most of the participants were arrested.

The Sugar Mill was a popular shopping center.

Sullivan Drugs was originally located at 210 South Adams, they later moved to the corner of Miccosukee and Magnolia. A Walgreens stands there today. Mr. Sullivan was always ready to help and would come down and open his store if you needed a late-night prescription.

Sunset Fish Camp operated by Ray & Nancy Mustart, was located on the north side of Lake Jackson and was a favorite spot to launch your boat to fish. When the waters receded in the lake the camp found itself land locked.

Sweet Shop across the street from FSU at 701 West Jefferson Street was a popular spot for college kids to meet and hang out.

Swimming pools Tallahassee originally had two pools, one at Levy Park and the other at Myers Park. Because it was a segregated city the pools were "white only." Under threat of a lawsuit against the city by black leaders a "colored" pool was opened May 9, 1953 and named Robinson-Trueblood. The pool was named after Army Private Eddie Robinson and Captain David Trueblood, the first black men from Tallahassee to be killed in the Korean War. The pool was built in response to wade-ins by blacks at all-white pools. During segregation, it was the only pool where black residents could swim and train as lifeguards.

Supreme Ice Cream had a distribution plant at 1103 South Adams. They billed themselves as "The South's Finest Ice Cream." The plant was managed by Wayne Cook.

T

Taft's Drive –In located directly across from the Capital Drive-In Theater had great barbeque. They said, "*Just toot your Horn,*" and offered dine-in or curb service.

Tallahassee Airports Tallahassee has had three municipal airport locations. Prior to opening a municipal airport, a field where today's Governor's Square Mall and Indianhead Acres is located was used.

Dale Mabry Field named after Captain Dale Mabry a WWI hero who perished when the air balloon *Roma* hit a power line on its test flight. It was a dirt field off of West Pensacola opened November 10, 1929. In World War Two the site was used by the military as a base to train pilots. The location today is the campus of **Tallahassee Community College**.

Tallahassee Municipal Airport off of Capital Circle was opened March 29, 1961 and served Tallahassee until 1993.

Tallahassee Regional Airport was opened December 23, 1989.

Tails & Tweeds was where you went to rent your tuxedos for the prom. Located at116 East Pensacola Street, they later moved to the Tallahassee Mall.

Tallahassee Community College started in the new Godby High School building on Tharpe Street. First classes were held Sept 21, 1966. They later moved to the old Dale Mabry airfields on Appleyard Drive.

Tallahassee Democrat –First started as the *Weekly True Democrat* by John Collins. The first edition was published March 3, 1905. Second owner Milton Smith turned it into a daily afternoon delivery paper in 1915 changing the name to the *Daily Democrat.* In 1925 the paper was called the *Tallahassee Daily Democrat;* the *Tallahassee* part was dropped in 1929. The 1929 Sunday paper was called the *Sunday News-Democrat.* The name was officially changed to the *Tallahassee Democrat* July 31, 1949. The paper was converted to a morning newspaper Jan 1, 1978. Offices have been at the northeast corner of College Avenue and Collins 1905 to 1909, 115 S. Adams (currently the Doubletree) from 1909 to 1953, 100 E Call 1953-1968, and 227 N. Magnolia- May 6, 1968 to present. Memorable writers; Malcom Johnson's *"I Declare,"* Bill McGrotha's *Sports*, Dorothy Clifford's *Capital Scene,* Ashby Stiff *Food Critic*, and Mary Ann Lindsey and Gerald Ensley's *Opinions.* Readers loved, hated or tolerated them.

Tallahassee Federal Savings and Loan on North Monroe provided the time and temperature phone service for Tallahassee. When you dialed their number you would hear *"Time flies and your money piles up when you open a savings account at Tallahassee Fede*ral" then the correct time and temperature would be given. They told prospective customers to *"Go where your savings grow — Tallahassee Federal Savings and Loa*n."

Tallahassee Little Theater started February 10, 1949. In 1952 the Winthrop's donated 3 acres of land for their first building located on the corner of Betton and Thomasville Roads

Tallahassee Mall opened 1971. Some early stores were Gayfer's, Woolco, Service Merchandise, Stafford's Jewelers, Hickory Farms, Tinder Box, and Morrison's (later Piccadilly's.)

Tallahassee Memorial Hospital opened Nov 4, 1949 and offered 150 beds. Prior to its opening Tallahassee residents were dependent on Archibald Memorial in Thomasville or the Edwards TB Hospital on Gadsden Street.

Tallahassee Motor Hotel and Dining Room was located on Monroe Street across from Lake Ella. The dining room boasted it was *"A good place to eat!"* Manny's Restaurant occupied the old restaurant after the motor hotel closed.

Tallahassee Music Scene through the years has gone from records to trios, combos, and bands. Some notables: Glen Lee, The Webb's, Velvets, Marauders, Midknights, La Bamba, Kidnappers, The 8 of Us, Esquires, Brand Brothers, Sonics, Mystics, Grant Peeples, Tallahassee Band, Tom & the Cats, Velma Frye, Pam Laws, Rita Coolidge, Jim Morrison, Eli, Cypress Creek, Crosscut Saw, The Reasons Why, Slut Boys, Cannonball Adderley, and Hutch & Hoss to name but a few. It's all good!

Tallahassee Police Department was located on Park Ave adjacent to City Hall. There was a holding cell in the back. A new building was constructed on Seventh Avenue in 1972 on the site of the former Sealy Elementary School. I remember before it was completed watching the 4th of July fireworks from the building in 1971. The old police station has housed a gay bar and a coffee house since the cops moved out.

Tallahassee Radiator Shop at 1423 North Monroe is one of the older surviving businesses in Tallahassee. Started by Henry Trammel (*Henry the Radiator Man*) they still repair radiators in the same place off of North Monroe near the Tallahassee Police station.

Tallahassee Tiger Sharks were the cities attempt at a minor league hockey team in 1994. They lasted seven years, until 2001.

Tallahassee Tumbling Tots was the name for a group of gymnasts organized in 1949 by Dr. Hartley Price. The program was taken over by the Tallahassee Parks and Recreation Department in 1953. They reached some fame in the early 1960's when they appeared six times on the Ted Mack Amateur Hour and later the Mickey Mouse Club. They were also featured in National magazines. Before other facilities were built, they used to practice at the old armory and later downstairs at the Northwood Mall.

Tallahassee Waterworks was the city water facility built in 1890 to supply water to the city. Water was pumped from a pond that was located near today's Myers Park. A newer facility to replace the wooden building was built in 1904 and stands today on the corner of East Gaines Street and Gadsden. Many plans have been made for the site but nothing has come of them as of yet.

Talquin Inn was one of the two or three favorites of legislators and locals. Run by the Taylor family they specialized in steaks and seafood. They offered private rooms for dining parties. Because the county was dry, patrons had to BYOB (Bring Your Own Bottle). The restaurant would then supply "set-ups" of ice and mixers. It was located on the "*New*" Quincy Highway at 2759 West Tennessee Street by the railroad overpass.

TALQUIN INN

AIR CONDITIONED

Sea Foods

STEAKS

ITALIAN SPAGHETTI
A SPECIALTY

OPEN
5 PM Til 1 AM
Monday Thru Saturday
Closed Sunday
Private Dining Rooms

FOR RESERVATIONS

599-9427

2759 W. TENN
3 Mi. West on U.S. 90 and Fla. 20

Tasty Pastry at 629 West Tennessee Street was a doughnut shop that also supplied J.M. Fields bakery when they opened. Their glazed doughnuts were some of the best.

Tempo Lounge at 1426 West Tennessee was a popular watering hole for workers wanting to unwind. Located in front of the Jitney Jungle Store on West Tennessee Street, **Good Time Charlie's** later opened there. The building is now occupied by a **Firehouse Subs**.

Terry Rosa Hardware at 1429 South Monroe was started by Herman Terry and brothers J.R. & Bill Rosa. They sold it when they went into the service in 1943. It has been serving Tallahassee for years.

The Office was a bar located at 1321 South Monroe down the hill from the capital. You could always tell the truth when you said, "I've been at the office all day."

Thomas Chevrolet operated by Bill Thomas, son of Tommy Thomas from Panama City, was on the corner of John Knox and N. Monroe. Bill was involved in serving the community by sponsoring the annual fireworks and Thanksgiving dinner give-away. He and his sister used to appear in the Tommy Thomas Chevrolet commercials in Panama City. We watched both of them grow up in those commercials. "*See the USA in your Chevrolet.*"

Thompson's Hamburgers is the name most remember for the Thompson's Snack Bar located at 1319 South Monroe. Before there were What-a-burgers in Tallahassee there were Thompson burgers, such big man-sized burgers that most could only eat one.

Tilman's Gift Shop was located at 101 East Jefferson.

Time of Day and the temperature was offered by Tallahassee Federal Savings and Loan. The phone number was first 2-5510, later 118, and finally 222-5510

Tony's Pizza was one of a couple of pizza joints in Tallahassee in the 1960's. Located at 1805 Thomasville Road; their motto was "*Pizza to go in just seven minutes.*"

Trampolines in the early 1960's there was a place off of the Apalachee Parkway next to the Parkway Bowl that had trampolines set in pits in the ground. For nominal fee for a half hour or hour time limit you could come and jump to your hearts content.

Trash men or *"garbage men"* used to come around behind your house to empty the trash. Before plastic trash receptacles they would dump the trash into their big white oak woven baskets that stood about four-foot-tall, then drag it to the street to dump in the garbage truck.

Trinity Methodist Church at corner of Park Avenue and Duval was rebuilt in the 1960's. Prior to that the old church had stood on the same location since 1840.

Trot-A-Way Club was a horse stable located on St. Augustine Road where the Centel Telephone office is now located.

Troxler's Boy's Wear at 212 South Monroe catered to the young men in Tallahassee.

Tuckers Drive-in at Four points offered fried chicken in a box. You could eat it there or take it with you.

Turner's was a woman's store located downtown at 116 South Monroe.

Turtle's was a music store located in the old grocery store building where the city of Tallahassee Bus terminal is today.

U

Union Bank Florida's first bank built in 1833 was located on Adams Street next to the Columns, and where the First Baptist Church is located today. It was moved to its current site (home of a former Standard Oil station) on Apalachee Parkway a block down from the Capitol on October 19, 1971.

USS Tallahassee Bell from a ship named after the city (formerly the Florida) used to be located in the horseshoe parking lot behind the old Capital building and in front of the Florida Supreme Court building. It was removed and placed at the Columns when they were constructing the new capital building.

V

Vanity Boot Shop 114 East College sold women's shoes.

Van Brunt & Yon at 905 West Gaines was a hardware store in town for many years.

Vason's Jeweler's was located at 124 East Pensacola.

Vardi's was Tallahassee's first boutique. It was located in an old house at 214 West College Avenue

Varsity Grill was located at 301 East College in the 1950's.

Varsity Theater was located at High Road and Tennessee Street. It later became a Muggs and Movies.

Velda Ice Cream at 1103 South Adams was managed by Wayne Cook.

Velda Dairy on Thomasville Road is now a Tallahassee subdivision.

Vogue Cleaners at 1839 Thomasville Road opened in 1961. It was run by George and Margaret Slager.

San Luis Mission Marker on Monroe & Brevard

W

Walker Library was originally located at the corner of Monroe and East Park Avenue and was called the *"University Library."* In 1903 the library was moved to a building at 209 East Park Avenue. Named for former Florida Governor David S. Walker. This private library was organized in 1883 and was Tallahassee's first library. It operated as a library until 1976 when it was placed on the National Register of Historic Places.

Inside Walker Library

WTAL Radio *"1270 on your dial"* was the first radio station to begin broadcasting in Tallahassee. The station was located in a house on the corner of Betton and Thomasville Road. It went on the air October 7, 1935. The property and building was later purchased by the First Baptist Church as a mission plant to start the **Thomasville Road Baptist Church**, constructed in 1954. Thomasville Road Baptist moved down the road near 1-10 in 1978 and the old church building became

The Haystack, a retail store. Today a number of shops are located there.

WCTV Channel Six located at 2225 North Monroe was Tallahassee's first television station. It began broadcasting September 15, 1955. For many years the only station available locally was Channel Six, later if you had good rabbit ears or an outside antenna you might get the Panama City station or the one out of Albany, Georgia.

WCTV stands for **W**e're **C**apital **T**ele**V**ision. It was initially an NBC affiliate.

Famous WCTV personalities included:

- Newsman Frank Pepper, the brother of Florida Senator Claude Pepper.

- Willie Ragsdale aka "Willie the Weatherman

- Anna Johnson who hosted the Good Morning Show

- Miss Carolyn Hagen who hosted the Romper Room where she would stare into her looking glass at the television to see who was being a good boy or girl.

- Roy Lamere who did the morning Farm Report.

- Jack Ridner hosted an afternoon kids program called the Circle 6 Ranch. Kids would go there for birthday parties. *"Captain Jack"* or *"Foreman Jack"* as Ridner called himself would hand out signed pictures of himself atop his rearing horse to the children. If a kid went to any IGA store and told them "I'm a Buckaroo!" they would receive a free sucker courtesy of Channel Six.

Jack Ridner

- Frank Ranicky took over in 1972 from Frank Pepper. Ranicky retired in 2008.

- Babs Wilhoit was another long time WCTV personality.

Wagon Wheel Drive-In called Freeman's Wagon Wheel or Ted's Wagon Wheel was located south of the Capitol at 2411 South Monroe and boasted of their fried chicken being *"Southern Fried"* NOT Roasted-NOT Broiled.

Walker Rabbit Easter Egg Hunt was a feature started by Tallahassee Democrat Editor Walker Lundy. Clues to an Easter basket hidden by *"Walker Rabbit"* were given in the Easter Sunday edition of the paper. Clues would take the treasure hunters all over downtown Tallahassee seeking clues for the telephone number to call to win. Whoever solved the puzzle first and called in won. Many an Easter Sunday was spent searching for the prize basket.

Walter Cronkite was the news anchor for CBS news. Because Tallahassee only had one television station for years, we all grew up learning what was going on in our world from him. He told us of the Cuban Missile Crisis, the Kennedy and King assassinations, the Vietnam War, man landing on the Moon, and the resignation of President Nixon. He would sign off with *"and that's the way it is"* and the date. He started as the CBS news anchor April 16, 1962 and retired March 6, 1981.

What-a-burger had two locations in Tallahassee. One was on the corner of Tennessee Street and Ocala Road but has been torn down to make way for a Publix Shopping center. The other still operates at Thomasville Road and Fifth Avenue.

Wescott Building was built on what was known as Gallows' Hill, site of former College Hall built there in 1854.

Western Auto was located on Monroe Street between Call Street and Park Avenue.

Wheelers Building Supply on Gaines Street was one of a couple of lumber supply places on Gaines Street for many years.

Whites IGA or Willis Grocery was across from Leon High School at 501 East Tennessee. There was also another Willis Grocery at 517 West Gaines Street.

Whittles offered pony rides on Thomasville road. Anyone who grew up in Tallahassee in the 50's and 60's either had their birthday party there or went to someone else's there. The ponies were attached to a turnstile-like frame big enough for four horses. Kids would mount up and Mrs. Whittle would lead the ponies around in a circle.

Wicker Picker was a home décor store that opened in the Tallahassee Mall in 1981. It closed in 1990.

Willis Dairy stores on Tharpe Street and Jackson Bluff Road sold milk and juice out of their small drive-up stores.

Eli Witt Tobacco & Candy Co. sold wholesale to local stores. They were located at 422 North Duval Street.

P.W. Wilson's was a woman's shop located at 204 South Monroe. They used an air tube system like you see at some banks to send cash and receipts upstairs to their head accountant.

Woolco Department store was located in the Sugar Mill Plaza.

F. W. Woolworths at 120-26 N. Monroe Street was located next to the Florida Theater. You could go to their candy counter and buy a white bag full of your favorite candy to take to the show. They also had a lunch counter that was made famous in 1960 during pre-integration times when black students from Florida A&M staged a sit-in there demanding to be served.

X

Madame X the name given to the mysterious woman who was Gov. Claude Kirk's date and who became his future wife Ericka.

Y

Yates Furniture Co. at 710 North Monroe.

Y2K stands for year 2000. State offices in Tallahassee spent time and money preparing for the advent of the year 2000 worrying that all computers were only programed through 1999. Turned out there was nothing to it.

Yum Yum Donuts was located on Apalachee Parkway and always had delicious treats.

Z

Zabenko Piano House at 1341 Jackson Bluff Road.

Zip codes were first used in 1963 and generally became accepted by the public in 1967. Tallahassee was divided into 11 zones 32301- 32311.

Sears on Monroe   Sears on Parkway

Talquin Inn   Capital City Bank

Studebakers   Brown Derby

A Timeline of Tallahassee Through the Years

1824 City of Tallahassee is established

1825 A Tallahassee Land Grant was given to Revolutionary War Hero General Lafayette.

1830 Union Bank established.

1833 Leon Hotel between Monroe and Adams opened.

1834 Tallahassee Railroad from Tallahassee to St. Marks constructed.

1843 Fire burned down most of downtown Tallahassee from Pensacola to Park between Adams and Monroe. City Council decrees only brick and stone can be used to build in downtown.

1845 Capitol building rebuilt after Tallahassee fire by Richmond A. Shine.

1854 & 1900 Voters statewide chose to keep the capital in Tallahassee rather than moving it to Gainesville, Jacksonville, or Ocala.

1861 Tallahassean's held a torchlight parade celebrating secession from the Union.

1865 Emancipation Proclamation read from the steps of the Knott House.

1869 First soda fountain opened at Lively's Drug store on Monroe St.

1877 Lake Ella named after May Queen Ella Bull by a suitor, was also called Bull's Pond.

1891 Tallahassee skyline changed with the addition of the cupola to the Old Capitol. First car on Tallahassee streets.

1898 Chain of Parks formally named. Area had first been developed when city was founded as a 200-foot-wide strip of land on Tallahassee's northern boundary as a defense against Indian attacks.

The seven Chain of Parks are: **Lewis** (between Gadsden and Calhoun)**Cherokee** (between Bronough and Boulevard) **E. Peck Green** (between Duval and Bronough) **Ponce de Leon** (between Monroe and Adams) **Bloxham** (between Monroe and Calhoun)**Randolph** (between Gadsden and Meridian) **McCarthy** also called Market Square or Waterworks Park (between Adams and Duval.)

1903 Street signs on downtown corners first appeared, Electricity first became available in Tallahassee.

1905 First long distance telephone service becomes available, University of Florida and FSCW created by legislature.

1905 Tallahassee Democrat began publishing.

1908 Governor's Mansion built.

1911 Supreme Court building begun.

1912 First permanent picture show opened on College Ave, first paving on city streets.

1914 first automobile taxi service began, City council adopted first speed limit of 10 MPH.

1915 first airfield (landing strip) carved out of a pasture which is todays Governor's Square Mall, First Baptist Church downtown built.

1919 Tallahassee adopted city commission/city manager plan of government.

1920 total county population 18,000- 5,00 in city.

1924 Centennial Field first opened for summer baseball games.

1925 Leon Hotel burned down.

1927 First Tallahassee skyscraper built; the Exchange Bank Building on Monroe St.

1929 First talkie movie came to town "Broadway Melody," Dale Mabry Field opened bringing the first commercial air service to town, Floridan Hotel built.

1932 Tallahassee voted to allow movies to be shown on Sundays.

1933 December 3 State Theater fire - was reopened September 27, 1934 as first air-conditioned theater.

1935 first radio station WTAL began operations.

1937 Leon High School building constructed. Students moved into the new building Sept 13, 1937. The Class of 1937 was first to graduate in the new school. The auditorium has 1212 seats.

1938 Night baseball began in Tallahassee.

1939 Lively Vocational School established.

1939 Leon's Concrete stadium built - sat 840. First undefeated football team was in 1940.

1940 Romulus Thompson formed the Leon High Marching Redcoats, they played at the inauguration of Governor Spressard Holland.

1940 referendum passed to establish Tallahassee Memorial Hospital.

1941 Black and white pilots, British and Chinese officers are trained at Dale Mabry Field.

1943 Bus station at Adams and Tennessee St. opened.

1946 Tallahassee Branch of the University of Florida (TBUF) started at FSCW with 507 men.

1947 Legislature dissolve's separation of genders at state colleges.

1947 FSU Flying High Circus began, FSCW officially became FSU.

1949 Dutch Kitchen was in the Columns building.

1949 Tallahassee fairgrounds land purchased- 140 acres.

1950 First Tallahassee mall- the Apalachee Parkway Shopping Center opened.

1951 FAMU Community hospital opened on FAMU campus.

1955 September 15- WCTV Tallahassee's first television station began broadcasting.

1957 Tallahassee Jr Museum opened.

1957 Apalachee Parkway completed.

1957 Lafayette Community Center opens.

1958 FSU-Fla play football for first time.

1959 Dade Street Community Center opens.

1960 Florida Theater burns March 26, reopens May of 1961 showing "The Big Show."

1961 Tallahassee Municipal airport on Capital Circle SW opens.

1963 County public schools began integration.

1963 Capital Circle- locally called the *Truck Route* officially completed.

1964 Palmer Monroe Community center opens.

1964 FSU beats Fla for first time.

1966 Oct 22nd Sims murders occurred.

1966 Tallahassee Community College began in wing of Godby High, moved to present location in 1967.

1967 Leon voters pass initiative to sell liquor by the drink- had been dry since 1904.

1968 March 23 - first Springtime Tallahassee parade.

1970 Northwood Mall opened.

1971 Passenger train service to Tallahassee ended.

1971 FAMU Hospital closes.

1972 Tallahassee Mall opened.

1972-73 I-10 opens in Leon county.

1973 FSU credited with starting the streaking fad.

1974 Silver Slipper on S. Monroe burned down, relocated to Northwood Mall. Closed in 2009.

1974 last May Day festival held. Had been begun by English settlers in 1844. First Queen was Mary Meyers, last was Cathy Ann Collins.

1976 Bobby Bowden hired as FSU football coach.

1977 Florida's new capitol building built. The new complex took up the former Waller Park that was between the old capitol and the Supreme Court building.

1978 Ted Bundy murders two FSU sorority sisters in Chi Omega house.

1978 Renegade and rider Chief Osceola make their debut.

1979 Governors Square Mall opens.

1981 New Donald L. Tucker civic center opened on land called Fish's or Fishers Green.

1982 Governor's Club opens.

1984 FSU band inaugurates the "War Chant" in loss to Auburn.

1985 Tallahassee Vietnam Memorial dedicated.

1985 demolition begins on Floridan Hotel.

1985 Musical Moon opens in old A&P building on E. Lafayette.

1985 Hurricane Kate hits Tallahassee just before Thanksgiving.

1986 Lighting hits the May Oak in Lewis Park requiring it to later be cut down.

1989 new Tallahassee Regional Airport opens.

1989 Dec 23, one inch of snow falls in Tallahassee – other snow dates Feb 1973 & 1958.

1993 Amtrak brings back passenger train service after 22-year absence.

1999 Lake Jackson drains, first time since 1982.

2000 Tallahassee the focus of the nation during 36-day presidential vote recount. George Bush declared winner over Al Gore.

2001- Space shuttle Columbia flies over the state capitol on the back of a 747.

Pick-up truck crashes into Jenny's Lunchbox.

2003 State of Florida hit by hurricanes Charley, Frances, Ivan, & Jeanne.

2006 Local Marine Lance Corporal Daniel Chaires killed in Iraq October 25.

2009 Bobby Bowden retires from FSU football. Mallory Horne only person to serve as Speaker of the House and Senate President dies. Gene Cox former Leon football coach dies.

2011 Miracle Theater on Thomasville Road closes is later replaced by Whole Foods.

2013 Leon High Principal Jim Nettles dies.

2014 Sheriff Larry Campbell dies.

2016 Hurricane Hermine hits Tallahassee.

2017 Gunman kills two, wounds five in shooting at Hot Yoga studio on Betton Road.

2018 Hurricane Michael hits Mexico Beach and the Forgotten Coast. Tallahassee affected as well.

2018 2000 disappearance of Mike Williams solved after 18 years. He was murdered by his best friend Brian Winchester in a scheme to be with his wife Denise Williams. In a plea deal Winchester got 20 years for testifying against Denise who was sentenced to life.

To the Reader:

I am sure after reading through this material your memory has been rekindled and there are places I have missed. By no means was this list intended to be all inclusive. If you have places that you think I need to add, email me at jkt416@gmail.com. I will try to add them in a later edition. Any comments or suggestions are welcome!

.